**ALSO BY MARIS KREIZMAN**

*Slaughterhouse 90210*

# I WANT TO
# BURN THIS PLACE DOWN

# I WANT TO
# BURN
# THIS PLACE DOWN

*Essays*

## MARIS KREIZMAN

*An Imprint of HarperCollinsPublishers*

FIRST EDITION

Designed by Jennifer Chung

Library of Congress Cataloging-in-Publication Data has
been applied for.

ISBN 978-0-06330582-3

25 26 27 28 29  LBC  5 4 3 2 1

FOR JOSH

<4 <4

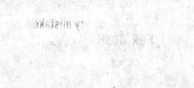

"When you find out who you are, you will no longer be innocent. That will be sad for others to see. All that knowledge will show on your face and change it. But sad only for others, not for yourself. You will feel you have a kind of wisdom, very mistaken, but a mistake of some power to you and so you will sadly treasure it and grow it."

—Lorrie Moore, *A Gate at the Stairs*

"This world is bullshit."

—Fiona Apple

# CONTENTS

# INTRODUCTION

Common wisdom has it that people grow more conservative as they age, that the proverbial "Deadhead sticker on a Cadillac" comes for us all. I'm the opposite, having moved further and further left with every year, growing more progressive as I, a straight cisgender white woman from a middle-class background, learn all the ways the world is rigged in my favor, even as I myself have been severely let down by the status quo.

The more I learn, the more mortified I am by the myths I once accepted as irrefutable facts.

For so long, I believed there was one correct path for my life, that having lots of academic and then professional ambition was the key to success, in whichever way I'd choose to measure success, money, or happiness. I believed that my job would love me back, that meritocracy existed, and that hard work was the key to fulfilling my every material and emotional desire.

I believed I'd own a home one day (I guess I'm still hoping), and that regularly contributing to a 401(k) would be all that was required to retire comfortably.

I thought that having Type 1 diabetes couldn't define me, that I should strive to be "normal," never mind the fact that I had to worry about my blood sugar all of the time. I certainly always thought that insulin would be available and affordable to anyone who needed it.

I thought there was a proscribed way to behave if you wanted to have successful romantic and personal relationships, and I believed that women's magazines could show me how. I thought that being skinny was a tremendously worthy goal, that beauty required pain.

I had little vocabulary to talk about sexual politics, so I thought that carrying a rape whistle and avoiding strange men skulking on the street late at night would keep me safe from harm.

I believed that abortion would always be legal in the United States.

I thought you should call the police if ever anyone was in danger.

I thought that labor organizing was impractical.

I thought that acid rain was the biggest threat to the environment, and that as long as we worked to close the hole in the ozone layer, our planet would be just fine.

I was wrong—about everything. I see now how unquestioningly I bought into the promises of democratic institutions that I later came to realize were at best deeply flawed, at worst irreparably broken. I didn't consider how enormously privileged it was to believe that such systems could work in the first place. The American Dream of my parents, and of boomers more broadly, has become less and less attainable for the next generation, and especially for the people who were never intended to dream such dreams in the first place: Black and Brown people, poor people, differently abled people, genderqueer people. And ultimately, these systems didn't even work out so well for me.

So here I am coming out as a late bloomer, a fortysomething former "good Democrat" who got angry and became radicalized and is stronger for it. Who finally has more faith in mutual aid than in government assistance. Who will never again donate to a national political campaign when there are people right outside my door I can help directly. Who is still actively choosing every day to break away from the self-centeredness of rugged individualism in favor of community and solidarity.

I want to share with you all the ways that I was wrong. Maybe you were wrong, too. Maybe we, together, can grieve what we thought the world was and hope for something better.

I WANT TO
BURN THIS PLACE DOWN

# SHE'S LOST CONTROL AGAIN

It's 1996, and I'm seventeen years old, lying on my bed on top of my yellow floral duvet, drenched in sweat. A police officer is standing over me, yelling for me to wake up. I see my parents huddled behind him in the doorway, looking terrified. I have no idea what's going on.

I don't remember the events that led up to this moment. Later, my parents will tell me that I had woken them to say that I was feeling strange. Then I passed out. Immediately, my mom injected me with glucagon, the quickest way to get my body the sugar it so desperately needed. Glucagon was only for emergencies; my parents had been trained to administer it, but they'd never had to use it before this morning. Still, I didn't stir. Their worst nightmare was coming true.

Now, all I know is that my pillow is damp and my skin is clammy and apparently the suburban New Jersey version of smelling salts is a cop gently slapping one's face. All you need to know is that I was safe at home with the people who love me most—and even so, I'd come as close as I ever had to never waking up again. And I was scared. We were scared.

———

It's the summer of 2020, and I'm reclining on the futon in the office-slash-guest-room-slash-storage-closet. I've closed the door because I'm on a video call with my psychiatrist, and even though I'm not particularly concerned that my husband will overhear through the flimsy walls of our apartment, it still feels odd to process my feelings out loud while he's in the next room. I love to complain about our small apartment, but I am so lucky to be safely inside with someone who is always up for a game of Scrabble or some *Seinfeld* reruns. We're actually having quite a bit of fun, which feels almost shameful during a time when so many people are suffering.

Halfway through our session my doctor asks me, on a scale of 1 to 10, what my level of anxiety has been over the last month. How to assign a number to such a thing? Usually I say it's around a 5 or 6—indicating a constant low-grade anxiety, nothing I can't handle. But today?

"I'd say I'm like a seven or an eight."

"Why do you think you're higher than usual?" she asks.

"I don't know." I begin to twirl a strand of my hair around my finger, my most notable nervous habit.

The past few weeks have been as level as they can be during a global crisis. Job stress is manageable, my parents are safe and healthy in New Jersey, and my relationship with my husband is a balm. Yes, the world is on fire, and I'm furious every time I look at the news or see vulnerable delivery people scurrying through the streets, making sure that those of us inside have what we need. But personally, I am so lucky. Take away everything else that might factor into my higher-than-usual anxiety number, though, and what's left is my blood sugar. It's always my blood sugar. Funny how I'm supposed to quantify my anxiety when all I do all day is think about numbers anyway.

"I keep waking up in the middle of the night with my blood sugar high," I say. "And I don't know why. I'm doing everything just as I've always done." More hair twirling.

Diabetes is a numbers game in which the goal is for one's blood sugar to remain in a given range as much as possible, roughly between 70 and 200 mg/dL. This means my life is a struggle to avoid being too low, which presents more immediate danger in the short term (as I experienced in my childhood bedroom), or being too high, which, over time, could lead to long-term complications like nerve damage and blindness. The parlance of diabetes relies heavily on moral judgments as descriptors of health. If you can regulate your blood sugar without "cheating" too much, if you can "be good" at eating well and making sure that your blood sugar is "normal," then ostensibly you should be "in control."

But that's not how diabetes actually works. No matter how strict I am, no matter how compliant and "good," there will still be times when my blood sugar is way the fuck outside of my control. I could eat the same food and take the same amount of insulin on a Monday and get one result, and then do the same on a Tuesday and get a completely different result. I've become good at predicting how insulin and food and exercise will affect my blood sugar, but I'm not always right, especially when there are other factors that are beyond my grasp. Sometimes it's as simple as ordering a Diet Coke at a restaurant and taking a few sips before realizing it's a regular Coke.

Then there are the things that happen inside my body that I am absolutely not in charge of. By now I've injected myself enough times that scar tissue has built up inside my body, and scar tissue impedes the absorption of insulin. So there are times when I unintentionally choose a bad injection site and my blood sugar ends up at 250 when I was expecting it to be 150 at most. Hormone surges can affect my blood sugar, and as any woman can tell you they're impossible to predict. Being ill makes my blood sugar high. In fact, all kinds of stress—physical and mental—have a major impact on how my body is able to process sugar. Being in control is such a simple idea. The word "control" implies that I have the agency to take the reins, to master my endocrine system. But no matter how determined I am, I inevitably have to deal with unexplained peaks and valleys. I am more than willing to put in the work to get the results I seek. Learning to live with uncertainty is the part I'm still no good at, even after a lifetime.

I was nine years old when my pancreas stopped making insulin and I was admitted to Monmouth Medical Center in Long Branch, New Jersey. While I stabilized, my parents learned all sorts of things—how to recognize the signs and symptoms of high and low blood sugar, what and when to feed me, how to cry discreetly without alarming me too much, how to "milk" my fingers once pricked in order to coax out an adequate amount of blood to test my glucose levels, how to give me twice-daily insulin injections in the fleshy part of my arm. There was a lot of practice that involved holding syringes like darts and stabbing oranges with them, quickly and without hesitation. Oranges remain my least-favorite fruit.

Back then, there was no way for us to know what I know now: that whenever a doctor makes a diagnosis of a chronic illness, the patient should automatically and immediately get a referral to a psychiatrist. Instead, I got a referral to a peer support group led by a nurse practitioner, where I experienced social anxiety while sitting in a circle on the carpet of a playroom with a bunch of other kids, trying to put into words all of the ways my life had irrevocably changed over the course of a few months. I didn't last very long on that floor.

As sunny as my doctors and educators had been about my future (they promised a "normal" life, and for the most part they were right), my diagnosis of Type 1 "juvenile" diabetes meant that I would always need to be hypervigilant about my health. No time off, no vacation days. And slowly arriving at that realization over time can make a patient feel anxious or depressed or angry, sometimes all of the above.

For an overthinker like me, the rise and fall of my blood sugar gives me endless fodder. I'm not sure if my diabetes was the cause of my diagnosis of OCD in later years, but it certainly didn't help. Every night before I turn off the light to sleep, I calculate how much insulin I need for the day. Below twenty units is good: it means that I didn't overeat, or that I wasn't overly stressed, or that I exercised, or that my body has chosen to behave. Over twenty units is bad: taking too much insulin regularly can make me sluggish, hungry. And so, except for a few moments before I'm fully awake, I have numbers running through my head at all times. So much so that the very act of regulating my blood sugar goes well beyond a healthy preoccupation and turns into something uglier.

So that now I'm playing with my hair, my favorite form of self-soothing, as my psychiatrist refills my prescription for my SSRI of choice.

———

IT'S 2022, AND I'M WATCHING A JOY DIVISION VIDEO ON YouTube, a rare live performance from September of 1979. The song is "She's Lost Control," and Ian Curtis is magnetic. He's quiet and measured in the studio recorded version of the song, but onstage, the tension builds and builds over three and a half minutes while Curtis does a frantic, frenzied dance that feels like a lead-up to a breakdown. As the story goes, Curtis had been so devastated by the news that an acquaintance of his died in her sleep during an epileptic seizure that he wrote a song about her.

Ian Curtis died by suicide in 1980 at the age of twenty-three. The brief and troubled life of the Joy Division front man has been the subject of much scrutiny, the kind of mythologizing that happens when a burgeoning rock star dies too soon.

In life, Ian Curtis was himself epileptic and prone to having seizures. I've read that he actually had seizures while performing onstage, but the only video I can find online is embedded in a scholarly journal called *Epilepsy & Behavior* that I've decided not to pay money to access.[*] There are some things I do not need to see. Instead, I watch a clip from a film in which Ian Curtis, as played by the actor Sam Riley, has a seizure onstage. It is a scary yet thrilling scene in which Curtis's convulsions feel both organic to the performance and entirely alien.

The clip is from a 2007 Ian Curtis biopic called *Control*. The film's director, Anton Corbijn, told the *Guardian*[†] that it takes its title from Curtis being "something of a control freak, although

---

[*]  Mia Tuft, Bergljot Gjelsvik, and Karl O. Nakken, "Ian Curtis: Punk rock, epilepsy, and suicide," *Epilepsy & Behavior* (November 2015): 218–21.
[†]  Paul Lester, "It Felt Like Someone Had Ripped Out My Heart," *Guardian*, August 2007.

the one element in his life that he couldn't control was the epilepsy." I saw the film once before, many years ago, with a man who often made me feel out of control in a different way.

———

IT'S 1988, AND I'M WALKING, WALKING HARDER THAN I'VE ever walked before. I've just turned ten years old, and today, my parents and I are walking in the fundraising walkathon for the Central Jersey chapter of the Juvenile Diabetes Foundation (JDF). We're joining hundreds of other people who will walk six miles along the boardwalk in Asbury Park, New Jersey, up through Spring Lake, and back. There will be rest stops along the way, spread out every few miles, so walkers can refuel and rehydrate, and so diabetic kids like me, whose bodies are burning sugar more quickly than normal, can feast on chocolate with no judgment.

We reach the first rest stop, and my mom turns to me. "Ooh, look what they have," she says, holding up a Baby Ruth from a snack table that also features among its offerings bananas and apple juice and peanut butter crackers.

She hands it to me, and I tear it open, eating half of it more quickly than I ordinarily would, knowing that it's the rare occasion in which there is no need to savor.

"They couldn't spring for a Snickers?" I say, only half joking. I would say the weak B-level candy (c'mon, it's no Snickers) is only a minor disappointment, but here I am writing about it more than thirty years later.

If candy is the short-term enticement, my parents and I and so many of the people who take part in the walkathon are also lured by the promise of a cure. People speak of a cure for AIDS and cancer as if they might be on the immediate horizon, as if some doctor somewhere will invent a special shot that all patients will be able to access and then immediately regain their health. So why not hope for the same in imagining a world without diabetes? For years, the name of the fundraising event was Walk for the Cure, but today it's called Breakthrough T1D Walk, Jersey Shore. At some point the organization must have realized that they were overpromising. Years later I would read Ann Patchett's *State of Wonder*: "Hope is like walking around with a fishhook in your mouth and somebody just keeps pulling it and pulling it."*

I feel the beginnings of a charley horse emerging in my calf as I shove the rest of the Baby Ruth into my fanny pack for later. I will feel the physical efforts of the day for weeks to follow, each pang of hamstring soreness making me feel accomplished, as if you could measure what I'd be willing to do for a cure by how much I'd sweat. It's like my parents and I believe in some bootstraps-loving genie who will grant us a cure only if he is satisfied that we've worked hard enough for it. My parents and I are nothing if not proactive. We grasp at any action that might give us some semblance of agency, and so we walk hard.

The twelve-mile slog is the easy part of the walkathon. Fundraising is the part that can make you bone-tired. For weeks before the event, I gathered up my courage and rang doorbells throughout my neighborhood, delivering a speech about how the listener's spare change could make my life, and the lives of other

---

* Ann Patchett, *State of Wonder* (New York: Harper, 2011), 49.

diabetics, so much better. My devoted, hardworking father wrote letters to friends and business associates stressing the importance of their generous donations in helping JDF to sponsor research and eventually find a cure. After the walk, I will write thank-you notes to the people who donated. Something like "Your donation has made my life a little bit sweeter." The funds Dad raises for JDF entitle us to a Sharper Image gift card, which he generously gives to me.

In October of 2021, a photo will circulate of a disastrous ocean fire in the Gulf of Mexico caused by a leak in an underwater gas pipe.* It looks like what I imagine the End Times will look like, like something out of an environmental horror movie. In the corner of the photo is a small boat, spouting a meager flow of water that is meant to help mitigate the fire but is so small and so far away that it makes no impact whatsoever. I understand the impulse of the people on that boat, the need to *try*, even if the solution, and, hell, even the problem itself, are way beyond their grasp.

———

IT'S 2021 AND I'M SITTING IN THE DINING ROOM OF KYU AT four in the afternoon, the only time we could get a reservation. It's our wedding anniversary, and we're newly vaccinated and on vacation for the first time in years. Josh and I could think of no better way to celebrate four years than to gorge ourselves at our favorite restaurant, a fancy Korean barbecue place in Miami's

---

* Maria Cramer, "Leaky Gas Pipeline Sparks an Inferno in the Gulf of Mexico," *New York Times*, July 3, 2021.

Wynwood Arts District, where reservations are hard to get, but where meats and vegetables are plentiful. We have ordered a feast: duck breast with crisp burnt ends; Korean fried chicken with a chili butter dipping sauce that is the ideal blend of savory and spicy; roasted broccoli cooked to such perfection that even as a vegetable, it still counts as a treat. I sip my cocktail, some tequila drink recommended by our server as "not too sweet." When she brings out the cocktail, it is an unexpected bright green color and tastes a little sweeter than I would have liked, but that doesn't faze me.

I put my glass down and look around surreptitiously to make sure that no one is nearby.

"Cover for me," I say, and Josh obliges, knowing it's his job to warn me if a server or anyone else is approaching our table.

With Josh on the lookout, I take out my insulin pen, dial up a small extra dose, around four units, hold the cap in my mouth because there's nowhere else to put it, lean my arm on my knee and surreptitiously inject myself in the fleshy part of my arm. I'm an expert at this. It takes five seconds, tops.

The first course arrives, and we cut a gooey burrata in two. It looks slimy but tastes divine, and I use a small piece of bread to mop it all up. An auspicious start! And yet I'm starting to feel strange.

Our server clears our plates, and I look at my phone. Of course I know it's rude to pull out my phone during a meal, but I have a better excuse than most. I have a handy new tool for monitoring my blood sugar that's as easy to access on my phone as my Twitter feed. And just like my Twitter feed, it can be informative and edifying, but more often than not, it is soul-crushing and addictive. It's called a continuous glucose monitor (CGM). Every ten days I inject a tiny sensor just below my skin and tape the transmitter that's attached to it onto the back of my arm. With this slightly bulky appendage, I'm able to know my blood sugar at all times without having to do any finger pricks. Most importantly, my CGM has an alarm that goes off if my blood sugar get too high (I've programmed the high alarm to a tone called "tacata," which Josh says sounds like game show thinking music) or too low (that alarm is more like a nuclear meltdown warning, which is both terrifying and handy when it sounds in the middle of the night).

The rub about being able to check my blood sugar anytime I want to (rather than the six or seven times a day I used to check it when I had to use a drop of blood from my finger) is that I . . . do. I'll watch my CGM to see how my blood sugar responds while I'm eating meals; I'll keep one eye on it while I'm reading or watching TV.

I'll look in on my CGM when something upsets me to watch my blood sugar skyrocket (what a surreal experience to be able to watch the impact of stress hit me in real time). You know that feeling you get when you've just received bad news and your body feels tingly and sweaty in a bad way? That feeling can cause blood sugar elevation. Same goes for good news, or the anticipation of something exciting, like doing a live event with an author at a bookstore. The nervous energy that would otherwise invigorate me somehow alchemizes into high blood sugar.

My CGM updates every five minutes. There is always new information to take in, and I'm addicted. How many times a day did I look at my phone before this app? It can't have been a flattering figure. How much worse has it gotten with my CGM? What percentage of my time is spent checking its readings? Great, more numbers running through my head as I try to calculate how risk-averse and bad at breaking routines I was to begin with, and how much more severe those tendencies are now.

I wonder if it's still called doomscrolling if it's not social media you're looking at.

I haven't even eaten a bite of the clay pot rice dish with big chunks of crab that was highly recommended to us, but already my blood sugar is 180, as high as if I'd already finished my meal rather than just starting. And the arrow on my CGM indicates that it's increasing at a rapid clip. I silence my phone. No need to disturb fellow diners with the impending alarm.

"I'm high," I tell Josh. Wild how those two words denote the pinnacle of enjoyment for my weed-smoking friends. For me, it's torture.

I have tried for more than thirty years to articulate how my body feels when my blood sugar is high, but I can never get it quite right. I suppose I should try again here.

Imagine a mild case of the flu, with fatigue and aches but no fever. And yet, if you're anything like me, you feel strangely warm. Your skin might even flush. But along with the physical tumult, there is the panic, the anxiety of knowing that your blood sugar is high and that you can't do anything in the immediate moment about it. Even the fastest-acting insulin takes around twenty minutes to start working. So you're anxious that your blood sugar is high, and that anxiety then makes your blood sugar even higher. Quite the vicious cycle.

I begin to chug water; dehydration can be a culprit.

"What can I do?" Josh says. I know he would do anything for me, but there's literally nothing he can do right now.

"Nothing. I'll just take more insulin." And so Josh once again looks out while I dig up my insulin pen and take four more units.

The next course arrives, an appetizer of pork cubes that are perfectly seasoned and crispy on the outside but melt in your mouth. Here I am, feeling uncomfortable and ashamed, but for a brief moment I forget my angst to eat rapturously. This is easier to do because the fattiness of the pork should theoretically slow down the absorption of sugar in my blood. Win/win.

"Damn!" we say to each other. "Holy shit."

No sooner do we put down our forks than I pick up my phone again. I'm alarmed to see that my blood sugar is now 260, despite the four doses of insulin and the fat I've just consumed.

After all these years, a high number still feels like a moral failing. Even if you know better, it's as if being too high is the result of being undisciplined, of not paying close enough attention, of slacking off or eating too much cake. (Let me stop you right here to remind you that there's nothing wrong at all with diabetics eating cake occasionally, as long as there's enough insulin to cover it!)

Josh can see that I'm agitated, and he probably says something witty yet comforting, as he is wont to do. I feel so lucky to be here with him right now, there is literally nowhere else I'd rather be, and also I want to get up from our table and scream.

"Be present" is what we say to remind our addled brains to appreciate the physical here and now rather than dwelling on what's been or what might come. But I am unyieldingly stuck in my body at all times, so finely attuned to the way it feels that being present is exactly what I need to escape from. My body, especially with my CGM, tethers me to each individual moment in a way that feels oppressive.

I modify my menu for the rest of the meal. I order a dirty vodka martini because it contains very little sugar and mama needs a drink. I eat some creamed spinach and some exquisitely roasted duck, I skip the rice entirely and delight in watching Josh enjoy it. This would have been an occasion on which I would have allowed myself a rare dessert. But certainly no dessert today. I try to encourage Josh to order something. He refuses, ever loyal.

It takes hours for my blood sugar to finally come down, much longer than it should have. My hunch is that a slight sunburn, combined with dehydration, got me into this mess. But I'm still not sure. I wasn't in immediate danger, even when my blood sugar peaked at 325; high blood sugar feels awful, but it's not life-threatening unless I choose to spend most of my days at that level—and I wouldn't dare to do that! Instead, as ever, I would choose to act responsibly, by focusing on my body rather than my surroundings, by keeping my eyes down on the numbers on my phone.

I want to spend more time looking up at the world, particularly at my husband, preferably while we both eat dessert.

———

IT'S 2008, AND I'M WATCHING THE MOVIE *CONTROL* WITH A man who makes me feel out of control. He idolizes Ian Curtis, which is the most blatant of red flags and says a lot about his mental hygiene at the time. But I'm not going to tell you much more about this man, because this really isn't about him at all. It's about how he makes me feel: like I have no ownership over my emotions, like I am merely a sack of bones and feelings in service of someone else.

We have one of those overly emotional, clearly-toxic-from-the-outside romances that should have flamed out much earlier than it did—and would have, if we didn't also work together at a long-since-defunct digital media company, he in music, me in audiobooks. We sit in neighboring cubicles, yet still spend all day instant messaging. We are nearly inseparable. Our relationship is all-consuming, or at least that's how it feels from my end. When I'm not with him, I'm thinking about him. I endlessly re-hash arguments in my head like a bad earworm, one that I will eventually spend thousands of dollars on therapy and Xanax attempting to eradicate.

This is also the year I experience panic attacks for the first time. The relationship puts me in a perpetual state of fight or flight. He openly flirts with someone else in the office or says something unkind; a burst of adrenaline hits, and my body feels the way it feels when I have low blood sugar: racing heart, sweaty, weak and shaky, disoriented. But in actuality, my blood sugar is elevated. Highs feel like lows and vice versa. My signals are all mixed up.

One day, we are devastated to learn that a colleague of ours has died of a brain aneurysm. An HR rep who had gone to check in on him after he hadn't shown up to work for a few days discovered his body in his apartment.

Soon after, my on-again-off-again colleague and I go out with friends. He says something over dinner that makes me lose my appetite; I don't eat much. By the time I get home, around 1 a.m., after a couple of drinks and some crying in the dirty bathroom of a bar in Ditmas Park, I am relieved to get into bed alone and be done with the day. Sleep is a release.

But the next thing I know, it's bright out and I'm sitting on my couch in my pajamas, taking sips of Coke while my alarm clock blares. He is there, too, along with an HR rep. Wait, what? How the fuck did they get here?

It appears that this morning, I didn't wake up for work.

He explains that he got worried when he hadn't heard from me in hours—we are usually in constant contact. So he went and grabbed the HR rep and they raced to my apartment. I was apparently in a twilight state when my buzzer began to buzz persistently. Even though I'd clearly slept through my alarm, I somehow heard the buzz and managed at that point to get up from my bed and answer the door. I still don't know why I reacted to the buzzer but not the alarm. In my darkest moments, I am humiliated to think it may have been because I used to fantasize that he would come to my door one night, overwrought with equal parts shame and ardor, to declare his eternal love to me.

And now here he is in my home, along with a nice woman I barely know, watching me as I sit on the couch, trying to decide if they need to call 911. They don't. I'm coming to. As I slowly regain my ability to think and reason, I find the wherewithal to test my blood sugar. It's 45 (normal is around 80–120). I shudder to think how much lower it had been before they found me. Eventually they leave, and I sit on my couch in my sleep T-shirt and have a good cry.

Later in the day, I call my parents. I wish I could be the kind of daughter who is able to keep secrets, but I am hopeless at this kind of subterfuge. So I tell them that their worst nightmare almost came true once again. I've since learned there's a medical term for it: dead in bed syndrome,* when a Type 1 diabetic falls asleep and never wakes up. I know my dad has spent sleepless nights worrying about me alone in my studio apartment with no one to inject me with glucagon in an emergency. I don't know how to process the fact that I was saved by a man who treated me poorly, whose moods I could never predict, and whose small cruelties caused havoc in my own body.

———

IT'S 2018, AND I'M ON THE LIVING ROOM COUCH NESTLED under a PrimaLush throw blanket from Target, scrolling through GoFundMe. I've only recently heard that people—Americans!—are dying due to lack of access to insulin. This is news that goes against the story I heard as a kid, legendary among legions of diabetics, of how Frederick Banting,† along with two other inventors who discovered insulin, sold the patent to the University of Toronto for $1 each. They felt that insulin should be accessible to anyone who needed it. This was canon.

I search "insulin" on GoFundMe, and I see for myself the

---

* Jessica Jones, Steven James, Fran Brown, David O'Neal, and Elif I. Ekinci, "Dead in bed–a systematic review of overnight deaths in Type 1 diabetes," *Diabetes Research and Clinical Practice* 191 (September 2022).
† Julia Belluz, "The absurdly high cost of insulin explained," Vox, November 7, 2019.

pages and pages of diabetics begging for help. I later learn that at
least three American diabetics died from lack of insulin in 2018.[*]
The cost has gotten so high, so out of control, so unregulated (the
price of the kind of insulin I use increased more than 1,000 percent[†] between 1999 and 2019), that in 2019, *JAMA* reports that
one in four diabetics[‡] have to ration their insulin due to price. In
2021, I begin making a monthly donation to Mutual Aid Diabetes, a volunteer organization that directly supplies diabetes
medications and supplies to anyone who needs them. I make sure
to store expired insulin in my fridge next to the condiments rather
than throw it away, just in case I come across a diabetic person
who is in desperate need. And this does end up happening, a few
different times.

In 2024, after years of politicians from both sides of the aisle
touting the cost of insulin as a failure of whatever party was in
charge at the moment but doing nothing about it, regulation
finally happened, sort of. It took years of public pressure and
performatively angry tweets from Congress and the White
House, but finally the three major insulin manufacturers—Eli
Lilly, NovoNordisk, and Sanofi—agreed to cap insulin prices
at $35,[§] but only for those who have Medicare or private health
insurance.[¶] In other words, the companies did not cap the

---

[*]  Dr. Vikas Saini, "A Mother's Day Message to Pharma: Lower Your Insulin Prices," WBUR,
May 11, 2018.

[†]  S. Vincent Rajkumar, "The High Cost of Insulin in the United States: An Urgent Call to
Action," *Mayo Clinic Proceedings* 95, iss. 1, January 2020.

[‡]  Darby Herkert, BS1; Pavithra Vijayakumar, BA2; and Jing Luo, MD, MPH, "Cost-Related
Insulin Underuse Among Patients With Diabetes," *JAMA*, 2019.

[§]  Tami Luhby, "More Americans can now get insulin for $35," CNN, January 2, 2024.

[¶]  Will Weissert, "Biden sees a $35 price cap for insulin as a pivotal campaign issue. It's not
that clear-cut," AP News, April 21, 2024.

prices of insulin; they capped the copays. Access to insulin for Americans under sixty-five is still tied to employment. It is still the responsibility of the individual to secure a job with benefits that will enable them to be worthy of affordable insulin, which, postpandemic and in an age of a rising gig economy where fewer workers have access to healthcare, feels more difficult than ever. My insulin stockpile isn't going anywhere.

I used to fantasize about the day when I would have walked in enough walkathons to be cured of diabetes, of the ice cream sundaes I'd eat and the clearheadedness I'd experience. Now I understand that's not how it works. Many years after watching my parents put so much of their sweat into the Juvenile Diabetes Foundation, I learned that JDF, now called Breakthrough T1D, takes a great deal of money from the very same pharmaceutical companies that made insulin so unnecessarily expensive in the first place.* This is an unforgivable conflict of interest, a betrayal of all the patients the organization is supposed to be advocating for above all else.

Forget the cure; all I want is for all people who need insulin to easily be able to get it. There are no walkathons for that, only GoFundMes and mutual aid.

I've spent much of my life struggling with the idea that certain things will always be outside of my control, but I never thought that access to insulin would be one of them. I know I am so much more than my disease, as is every single diabetic person alive right now. When I look at GoFundMe, I see the faces of people who,

---

* Annalisa Van Den Bergh and Robin Cressman, "To End the Insulin Crisis, We Need to Divest from Diabetes Nonprofits," *Jacobin*, April 14, 2022.

through no fault of their own, have no control over their lives. The American healthcare system creates chaos for those without copious economic resources and with few support systems. If you're trying to make one vial of life-giving medication last for days or weeks, how can you think about anything else? The unregulated cost of insulin and all sorts of other diabetes drugs and tools (like my precious CGM) has created an entire generation of diabetic people whose lives are ruled by numbers that don't make any sense.

We all deserve to live in a world where diabetes is not a death sentence or a constant source of financial stress. At most, diabetes should be just an annoying thing that people like me will have to deal with every second of every day for the rest of our lives.

———

IT'S 2022, AND I'M EXFOLIATING. I AM NOT TRYING TO PUSH my multistep beauty routine onto you, I promise. Exfoliation of the skin on my arms is the first step in the process for inserting a new CGM sensor. Fresh from the shower, I avoid using any serums or lotions that could potentially cause my skin to be a less-than-perfect surface for medical tape to adhere to. I swab my arm with an alcohol pad, leaving plenty of time for it to dry so the skin won't sting when I pierce it.

It's been a bit of a learning curve, and there's a reason I've become so meticulous. The components of my CGM are expensive even with insurance, and they all have to be ordered through the mail. And yet, the adhesive comes unglued as if it were Scotch tape from the school supplies aisle of the pharmacy. There's much strategy involved in making sure it lasts.

I rest my arm on my knee so I can get to the back of it, the fleshiest area. I remove the adhesive from the sensor and place it very firmly against my arm, patting down the sides. Then I release most of the pressure. The sensor is meant to be injected just under the skin, and I've learned the hard way that it requires the lightest, gentlest touch. Press down too hard while injecting and you're likely to get a bleeder. Bleeders are messy in many ways, usually requiring the removal of the sensor and a call to the CGM manufacturer customer service to request a replacement to be mailed to you.

So, the gentlest touch. Once the sensor is in, I press the tape down again. Sometimes despite all my efforts the tape still doesn't lie completely smooth, and so I factor in a moment or two for cursing and muttering. Then I attach the monitor to the sensor and alert the app on my phone that we're ready to go. It takes two hours for the app to connect and to start showing me my blood sugar.

A few days in, a next step is required. There's a very thin layer of tape that I must put over the original tape, extra coverage to ensure that the CGM lasts for the full ten days. Affixing the tape requires two hands, so I enlist Josh to help. He's become quite skilled at it. Sometimes I wonder how I would have managed to affix that tape had I never met Josh, a year or so after I finally excised the other, toxic man from my life.

The numbers still run through my head even as my life improves in so many immeasurable ways: Josh and I move in together and adopt a grumpy old dog, I find work that is (at least a little) fulfilling, I get on the right SSRI and feel (slightly) more secure in my own body. The numbers don't care that I'm making personal progress; they're unmoved by drive and determination. I could do one thousand walkathons and it wouldn't matter; the numbers will follow me forever, no matter where I go and what I do.

# NEOLIBERALISM AND ME

The Meadowlands Sports Complex in East Rutherford, New Jersey. November of 1992. I'm newly fourteen years old, and I am at the biggest live show I have ever attended. Avid fans seem to have taken every single one of the stadium's 82,500 seats, and they're all buzzing with excitement. I've come with my parents, but no matter. I still feel like a grown-up simply for being in this audience where there are so few kids my age. Most everyone here looks like some version of my mom and dad: white, middle-class, enthusiastic.

We're here to see a superstar. Minute by minute, the anticipation builds as we wait for the headliner, the Mick Jagger of the night, our Axl Rose. Throughout the stadium there are fans chanting and clapping and waving signs. The energy is not dissimilar to those clips from the '60s of girls with bouffants weeping and losing their shit while the Beatles performed.

But aside from some highly publicized saxophone playing on late-night TV, the man we are waiting to grace the stage is not a musician. He just has the charisma of one.

It's the night before the presidential election and we are at a DNC rally and already I am a good future Democrat because I love Bill Clinton.

The man of the hour comes to the stage, and the place goes wild; confetti falls from the big domed ceiling. After what feels like ten minutes of rapturous applause, we quiet down in anticipation of his speech. A small hitch in the plan: after spending months campaigning all over the country, Bill Clinton has (literally) lost his voice. So in the end, he doesn't speak to us at all, beyond a few whispers: "My fellow Americans, this is a very big election, the first election since the end of the Cold War, the election that will chart our course into the twenty-first century,"*—instead letting Al Gore stand in for him, arguing for real social progress, and an end to (Republican) politics as usual in favor of policy that puts people first.† We also get to hear speeches from actors Glenn Close and Gregory Hines and Kathleen Turner and Richard Gere (fresh off sex work fairytale rom-com *Pretty Woman*!); being in the presence of Hollywood celebrity is thrilling. Then it's Hillary Clinton's turn, and she promises that all of us will be back on our feet again if Bill is elected. Then, to bring it all home, Michael Bolton sings "When I'm Back on My Feet Again."

I'm fourteen, so I can't entirely articulate what, specifically, needs changing in America, but what I do know absolutely is that Republicans, who've had a lock on the presidency for years, are evil and only care about other rich people and villainizing the poor. My parents have great faith that Bill Clinton will be the one to change all that, and I believe them. He's young and handsome; he's a Rhodes Scholar but also a man of the people; he's hip, or at least hipper than the Bushes. Tomorrow will be better

---

*    Gwen Ifill, "THE 1992 CAMPAIGN: The Democrats; Clinton Rallies Supporters for Final 'Long Walk,'" *New York Times*, November 2, 1992.

†    Clinton/Gore Campaign Rally, C-SPAN, https://www.c-span.org/video/?33343–1/clinton -campaign-rally.

than before, according to Clinton's campaign theme song, "Don't Stop," and I believe Fleetwood Mac, too.

Bill may be silent now, but his speeches have been playing on repeat every night on the news. "For millions and millions of Americans, the dream with which I grew up has been shattered," he said in a stump speech near Pittsburgh in April of 1992.[*] "The ideal that if you work hard and play by the rules you'll be rewarded, you'll do a little better next year than you did last year, your kids will do better than you. But that idea has been devastated for millions of Americans." Clinton promises that he will be the president to make "work hard and play by the rules" viable again, and I am a consummate hard worker and rule follower, so I have taken his messages to heart. I know that as long as he is elected, I will have the tools I need to succeed.

The evening ends with the cast of *Les Misérables* singing "One Day More," and I cry with the ardor of a French ragamuffin who feels entitled to a better life, who is certain that political change is imminent. America is headed for an era of post-Bush utopia, and I know that as long as I work hard and play by the rules, I will reap the rewards. I am sure anyone who chooses to do the same can do so as well.

———

IN 1996, FOUR YEARS AFTER THAT MEADOWLANDS RALLY, I mail in an absentee ballot to cast my very first vote in an election.

———

[*] Gwen Ifill, "Standard Campaign Speech: A Call for Responsibility," *New York Times*, April 26, 1992.

I vote to reelect Bill Clinton for a second term. I have just started college at the University of Pennsylvania, and finally, I feel like my hard work is beginning to pay off. To get here, I've done all the things expected of me: I got straight As in my final three years of high school, got great test scores, had well-rounded extracurriculars and after-school jobs. I took initiative. I am also a burgeoning feminist. In my government and politics class presentation senior year of high school, I argued that we must protect Roe v. Wade at all costs, not once thinking that it would ever be under serious threat. I was comfortable, and it was just a rhetorical exercise.

I believe that my admission to a good college will lead to a good job at a good company, which will then lead to personal fulfillment and a sense of purpose, along with adequate healthcare and eventual homeownership and plenty of money waiting for me in a retirement account. If I bust my ass over the next four years, I know I'll be able to enjoy some of those spoils.

Earlier that year, President Clinton invited one hundred business executives[*] to the White House to instruct these "good corporate citizens" on how they can "do well by doing good." Later, in 2022, Alex Pareene will explain this sea change in the *New Republic*[†]: "Unlike an earlier liberal consensus around 'doing well and doing good'—that is, growing the economy and providing for the downtrodden at the same time—'doing well by doing good' is a belief that there is no trade-off between making

---

[*] "Doing Well By Doing Good," *Time*, May 19, 1996, https://time.com/archive/6928723/doing-well-by-doing-good-3/.
[†] Alex Pareene, "The Disastrous Legacy of the New Democrats," *New Republic*, May 16, 2022.

money and improving the world, and in fact that making a lot of money is the best and most effective way to improve the world."

Good Democrat that I am, it doesn't occur to me that trusting America's largest corporations to care about the well-being of others is like trusting Hannibal Lecter to be satisfied by a dinner of a veggie burger with some fava beans and a nice Chianti. What could go wrong?

I am in the same graduating class as Donald Trump Jr. In college, he appears only to be a dumb frat boy with a bit of a drinking problem, not the legitimate threat to national security that he is destined to become. The only vaguely political thing I ever see him do during our college years is attend a protest on the College Green when the administration bans drinking at undergraduate parties in 1999 after a twenty-six-year-old alumnus of Donnie's fraternity dies after drunkenly falling down the stairs at their fraternity house.* (To be fair, I was at the protest, too.) I never gave Donnie enough credit; I've got to admit that he's really come a long way since then, political impact–wise.

Donnie is a Wharton student, just like his father was. I am at the College of Arts and Sciences, studying English with a concentration in dramatic literature. Most of my classes are held in Bennett Hall, a quaint old building that seemingly hasn't been updated since *The Great Gatsby* was published to mixed reviews. Donnie and his classmates at the business school have the richest donors and therefore the biggest, nicest buildings on campus, the most money to throw around, the most functional

---

* "University Sobered by Alumnus' Death on Campus," *Pennsylvania Gazette*, May 2, 1999, https://thepenngazette.com/university-sobered-by-alumnus-death-on-campus/.

air-conditioning, the most computer labs per capita (most of us in the late '90s have nontransportable desktop computers, so if you want to check your email before class you need to duck into a computer lab). Wharton is the crown jewel of Penn, and everybody knows it. But I, too, can take a few classes at Wharton—any undergrad can take up to three courses there, can access the knowledge of some of the best minds in business and learn some "practical skills" like marketing and branding to round out our liberal arts degrees. We are all encouraged to do so.

Donnie's presence at school sparks some cognitive dissonance, but I'm game for the mental gymnastics. I ultimately decide to view Donnie as a signifier of legitimacy, as if merely being in the same place at the same time as a kid whose entrance to college, among other things, has likely been purchased for him, is an indication that I am on the right path in life. As I brush by Donnie on the way to class, I am forced to revise my Clinton-inspired vision of how meritocracy works: Some rich and powerful people do get to buy their way into elite colleges. But I am able to interact with *those* people, whom I never would have met otherwise, because I've worked hard and earned it.

There's an entire literary genre called dark academia in which an outsider, maybe a little too naïve and idealistic, works their ass off to gain admission to an elite institution and gets caught up in the powerful insidery thrill of it all. Desperate to fit in, they distance themselves from their humble beginnings and take up the dramas and obsessions of their more privileged classmates. Such glimpses into the lives of the well-born and moneyed and blazered invariably and inevitably lead to disillusionment when

the outsider discovers the moral depravity that lurks not so far
beneath the shiny exterior.

Donna Tartt's *The Secret History* is the most famous example,
and it contains the whole checklist of the genre's hallmarks. In the
novel, middle-class Richard Papen of Plano, California, transfers
to an elite college in Vermont and falls in with a hyperprivileged
and hyperbrainy—and ultimately dangerous—crowd. My college
experience echoes the dark academia urtext in many ways. I go
to frat parties and learn more about lacrosse and try to fit in.
But instead of meeting people who are obsessed with beauty and
antiquity as Papen does in Tartt's masterpiece, the characters I
meet are obsessed only with having money and making more of
it in the future. Trade Hampden College's Classics for Wharton's
Management 102, trade Dionysian bacchanals for keggers and
2 a.m. shots of Jägermeister, trade the awe of encountering an
exquisite piece of art with the mania of following the peaks and
valleys of the stock market.

Even as an insecure teenager, I feel I am morally and intellec-
tually superior to them, these future investment bankers and tech
bros who want to make money above all else, who view art as a
distraction at best. Later, I will give them a slightly more chari-
table read: We live under capitalism. Why wouldn't they want
to accumulate wealth, when that's the clearest and most direct
way to measure one's worth within such a system? And that's
especially true for the strivers like me, who didn't start at the top,
who fought their way into a fancy school and wanted now to
remain there.

The most important lesson I learn in Marketing 101—a
prerequisite for business students and an elective for me—is

that so many of the students in my class are simply not sharp enough, not capable of sophisticated enough thinking, to be the kind of evil corporate overlord I imagined ran all of American business. It is when I meet some of these future kings of capitalism that I begin to consider what serial killers and CEOs really have in common: the American imagination gives them far too much credit for being diabolical, makes them out to be far more intelligent than they actually are. It is here where I learn how central mediocrity is to Hannah Arendt's concept of the banality of evil.

Here is what I remember about my first business school group project: five of us, grouped together by alphabet, tasked with choosing a company to analyze its marketing strategy. We choose to study Kohl's, the discount department store, because its 1992 IPO was a success; also, one of my classmate's parents has a friend who is high up over there and can get us some insider info. There is also a Kohl's located in Cherry Hill, NJ, not far from campus, so the five of us can take a field trip to study the actual customer experience.

Here is what I remember about my first business school group project, part two: I have to take over as group secretary because the classmate with the family connections to Kohl's, let's call him Trip, is so bad at it. Trip's meeting minutes are scattered, his notes grammatically incoherent, his scribblings indecipherable, even to himself. In fact, the first draft of our report now brings to mind that old David Foster Wallace chestnut from his essay in the *Oxford American Writer's Thesaurus* (2004), where he calls out people who use the word "utilize" when the word "use" is simple and direct and works just as well. Trip is a utilizer, delighting in making language more complicated than necessary in order to make his thoughts sound more complex. And yet the same guy who couldn't take proper notes radiates authority when making our presentation. So while I assume the pose of a dutiful executive assistant, Trip is all charisma, with no hint of stage fright. He almost makes me want to invest in Kohl's myself. Trip's performance requires an entirely different skill set from the ones I'd been trying to develop. A good work ethic is nothing compared to the inner confidence of a man who has never been taught to doubt himself and has no reason to consider that he might ever be wrong. (It is not until the year 2023 that I will hear the term "nepo baby" and it will all make sense.)

Here is what I remember about my first business school group project, part three: absolutely no details about the other three group members. I'm sure they don't remember me, either. I'm certain that Trip utilized all of the space in our collective memories.

Senior year, the Wharton students are in a tizzy, beginning to prep for interviews with investment banks like Goldman Sachs and Lehman Brothers, and consulting firms like McKinsey and Andersen and BCG—the Ivy Leagues of entry-level corporate jobs. Interviews for these companies are high-pressure, and you can feel the collective nerves mounting across campus. I see classmates reading books on how to ace the notorious case study, a key tool in consulting recruitment in which job candidates are asked to advise on topics they know nothing about. There are a bunch of these books, all of which emphasize how interviewees should handle uncertainty: namely, how to emanate expertise no matter how far adrift the subject. As I learned in my Wharton classes, some prospective bankers are more naturally talented in such performance than others. (Trip ended up in the mergers and acquisitions department of Goldman Sachs.)

In 2022, I would read *The Big Con: How the Consulting Industry Weakens Our Businesses, Infantilizes Our Governments, and Warps Our Economies*[*] and understand my college years in a new light. Authors Mariana Mazzucato and Rosie Collington lay out the terms of the case study interview: "Success in such exercises can be summed up as the ability to use superficial knowledge," they write. "And crucially, interviewers for such positions are not just looking for cognitive dexterity in a candidate's responses. They are often most keen to see self-assurance and conviction in the solutions the candidate proposes." In other words, the big consulting companies want recruits who are good at lying, and can do so with a smile. That's what they were teaching at business school.

I know it's wrong to portray an entire school, an entire field of study, as if it's made up exclusively of con artists. I'm sure there were smart, kind people who graduated from Wharton and who are now doing good in the world. There must have been. But when Donald Trump is your school's most famous grad, with his vile son in your class, it does tend to color how you perceive the rest.

———

* Mariana Mazzucato and Rosie Collington, *The Big Con: How the Consulting Industry Weakens Our Businesses, Infantilizes Our Governments, and Warps Our Economies* (New York: Penguin Press, 2023), 125.

IN SEPTEMBER OF 2000, I START MY VERY FIRST PUBLISHING job at a literary agency, a small division of a talent management company that represents athletes and models and other types who are nominally authors but who do not write their own books (ghostwriters are saints). At my very first meeting on my very first day of work, the company's billionaire CEO, who made his fortune representing the biggest golfers and tennis players of the '70s and '80s, turns red in the face and screams at me for not getting a message from him to my boss in a timely manner. (To this day, I prefer not to refer to a mixture of iced tea and lemonade as an Arnold Palmer, the name of this yeller's most famous client.)

I explain that it's my first day.

"That's no excuse," he yells. "With that attitude you're not going to last very long at this company!"

Did I mention he's the author of the book *What They Don't Teach You at Harvard Business School*, the marketing copy of which promises to reveal "the positive use of negative reinforcement"?

I burst into tears in front of all of my new coworkers, which is not a move any of my Wharton professors would have endorsed. They, in turn, say very little. I'm humiliated, but I vow to come back to work the next day and do better; I'm no quitter.

I like to portray myself as an innocent here, and certainly I had done nothing to warrant a public dressing-down on my first day of work, but here's where I confess that I took this job knowing that the agent who would be my boss had recently sold Jack Welch's memoir for $6.8 million. Yes, that Jack Welch. Neutron Jack. The man who was deemed brilliant for making General Electric the most valuable company on earth by moving away from manufacturing and toward "the blob," an amorphous collection of financial assets. According to David Gelles, author of *The Man Who Broke Capitalism: How Jack Welch Gutted the Heartland and Crushed the Soul of Corporate America—and How to Undo His Legacy*, Jack Welch destabilized the working class by closing factories and firing tens of thousands of employees, offshoring, and outsourcing.* Gelles sees a vastly different enduring legacy for the man who was once named Manager of the Century by *Fortune*: "[Welch] opened the door to an era where billionaire C.E.O.s are endowed with vast power and near total impunity."†

I entered the job market hoping to work for editors with stables of brilliant writers, but alas, my dream job at Alfred A. Knopf went to someone else. So instead, I'm working at this agency, mostly coordinating schedules for all of the various handlers involved in publishing celebrity memoirs. Jack Welch has a proper executive assistant, who has been with him for decades and who basically runs his life; my boss should probably have one of those, too, instead of some twenty-two-year-old who dreams of one day making art. Work consists mostly of excruciating boredom, punctuated with moments of high pressure. I'm an all-around bad fit. The tiniest of silver linings: Jack Welch's book publication date is September 11, 2001, and when his media coverage gets preempted by breaking news, he is furious.

———

* David Gelles, *The Man Who Broke Capitalism: How Jack Welch Gutted the Heartland and Crushed the Soul of Corporate America—and How to Undo His Legacy* (New York: Simon & Schuster), 2022.
† David Gelles, "How Jack Welch's Reign at G.E. Gave Us Elon Musk's Twitter Feed," *New York Times*, May 21, 2022.

I'M THREE MONTHS INTO MY TERRIBLE FIRST PUBLISHING job when Bill Clinton signs the Commodity Futures Modernization Act in December of 2000, a piece of legislation that deregulates derivatives trading—and paves the way for my former classmates and various other good liars to bring about the global financial crisis a few years later, punctuated by the collapse of Lehman Brothers and Bear Stearns in 2008.[*]

It turns out that many of my former classmates really are up to no good.

I'm on my second publishing job, in August of 2002, when I read that Arthur Andersen was found to have shredded documents during an SEC investigation into the fraudulent behaviors of the natural gas company Enron.[†] The company that only three years ago was considered "the Yale of consulting" on my college campus has shuttered.

Meanwhile, "the Harvard of consulting," McKinsey, is so notoriously and regularly evil that its Wikipedia page has its own Controversies section. Corporate scandals have plagued McKinsey throughout its existence, from "turbocharging"[‡] the opioid epidemic by advising Purdue Pharma on how to sell OxyContin, to supporting authoritarian regimes in China and Russia.[§] In 2013,[¶] the financial reporter Duff McDonald publishes a book called *The*

---

[*] Paul Blumenthal, "How Congress Rushed a Bill that Helped Bring the Economy to Its Knees," HuffPost, May 11, 2009.
[†] Mark Maurer, "Arthur Andersen's Legacy, 20 Years After Its Demise, Is Complicated," *Wall Street Journal*, August 31, 2022.
[‡] Michael Forsythe and Walt Bogdanich, "McKinsey Advised Purdue Pharma How to 'Turbocharge' Opioid Sales, Lawsuit Says," *New York Times*, February 1, 2019.
[§] Walt Bogdanich and Michael Forsythe, "How McKinsey Has Helped Raise the Stature of Authoritarian Governments, *New York Times*, December 15, 2018.
[¶] Duff McDonald, *The Firm: The Story of McKinsey and Its Secret Influence on American Business* (New York: Simon & Schuster, 2013), 8.

*Firm: The Story of McKinsey and Its Secret Influence on American Business*, in which he writes that McKinsey may be "the single greatest legitimizer of mass layoffs than anyone, anywhere, at any time in modern history." In 2023, McKinsey's revenues hit $16 billion thanks to a new focus on generative AI[*] products. It's difficult to see AI as anything other than the embodiment of the deficiencies of working hard and playing by the rules, with IMF managing director Kristalina Georgieva predicting in 2024 that AI will hit the labor market "like a tsunami."[†]

If Bill Clinton, my former hero, could so massively underestimate the lengths to which avarice thrives under capitalism, what else might he have been wrong about? What does it mean to be a good Democrat when Democratic policies are growing increasingly Republican? In their 2023 book *A Fabulous Failure: The Clinton Presidency and the Transformation of American Capitalism*, Nelson Lichtenstein and Judith Stein describe a litany of ways in which Clinton ushered a new wave of conservative leanings into the Democratic Party: "[T]he liberalization of trade, the deregulation of finance, the privatization of government services, the reductions of taxes on the rich, and the evisceration of the labor movement and the welfare state. That the Clinton administration embarked on this path is without doubt."[‡] I have to believe these policies would have sounded appalling to the majority of people who had watched the Clinton/Gore rally with

---

[*]  Lakshmi Varanasi, "McKinsey says it needs to reinvent itself and that AI is the answer: 'It's going to be most of what we do in the future,'" *Business Insider*, June 22, 2024.

[†]  Paulo Confino, "AI will hit the labor market like a 'tsunami,' IMF chief warns. 'We have very little time to get people ready for it,'" *Fortune*, May 14, 2024.

[‡]  Nelson Lichtenstein and Judith Stein, *A Fabulous Failure: The Clinton Presidency and the Transformation of American Capitalism* (New Jersey: Princeton University Press, 2023), 4.

me at the Meadowlands all those years ago, dreaming of something better.

In a country plagued by problems in which individual grit is not nearly enough to prevail over rotten systems, working hard begins to feel more like a Sisyphean task than a practical solution. Naomi Klein aptly sums up the false promises of neoliberalism in her excellent 2023 book *Doppelganger*: "In the neoliberal era that began in the 1970s and has not yet ended, every hardship and every difficulty—from poverty to student debt to home eviction to drug addiction—has been pathologized into a personal failing. Every success, meanwhile, is lauded as proof of the relative superiority of the supposedly self-made."[*]

——

By THE TIME I WATCH MY FORMER CLASSMATES' FINANCIAL institutions collapse in 2008—or almost collapse, and then recover due to enormous government bailouts—I am working at a start-up, where I've landed after being laid off from my most recent job in book publishing. In 2008, this feels like a safe move. Start-ups are the way of the future, and I am lucky to be rid of traditional book publishers as I move into a new and growing space with plenty of opportunity.

In the following years, I will work at a number of book-adjacent start-ups and, worse, corporations with divisions that are meant to "act like start-ups," which is just a way to allow for longer hours and

---

[*] Naomi Klein, *Doppelganger: A Trip Into the Mirror World* (New York: Farrar, Straus & Giroux, 2023), 231.

faster deadlines but with none of the flexibility. "Hardworking"
falls out of favor as the bootstraps adjective du jour. Now we are
meant to be "entrepreneurial," even those of us who just want to
write and edit well and get paid for it.

In the early aughts, it seems like anyone with an interesting idea
and a penchant for sleek design—and, last but not least, unfettered
access to VC capital—can start a business. It also helps to have a
penis. The founders of such companies are not worried about the
sustainability of these businesses. They assume growth will continue year over year for all eternity, a concept I now like to refer
to as the Founders Business Plan. I've only taken a few courses at
Wharton, but even I know that this is a revenue model that could
never work long-term.

Ambition within these start-ups is two-pronged: the true be-
lievers think they can make gobs of money *and* change the world.
They project a moral element onto start-up capitalism, as if the
act of selling things in a brand-new way could inherently be good
for humanity. Here we are, back to reinforcing Clinton's idea that
doing good and making money can go hand in hand. We have
learned nothing.

At the same time, a new kind of so-called rock star captures the
American imagination: the tech billionaire. Jeff Bezos decimates
the book industry and small businesses everywhere, then goes on
to receive glowing profiles about his business acumen and his
philanthropy and his love of books; meanwhile, his warehouse
employees piss in bottles because they don't get adequate bathroom breaks. Fellow Penn grad Elon Musk is hailed as a genius
and gets the Walter Isaacson biography treatment even as he busts
unions at Tesla plants and founds a company whose goal is to

merge human brains with AI—and this is before he tanked Twitter and started in on antisemitic rants. Mark Zuckerberg becomes the hoodie-wearing golden boy of the internet age, all while invading our privacy and spreading disinformation and inciting civil unrest. Not to mention all of the cryptocurrency hucksters and self-help gurus who cultivate adoring fandoms of their own.

Meanwhile, in my little corner of the world, the arts and media industry, private equity firms and media conglomerates are buying up websites and news organizations. Workers are stuck falling in line with corporate strategies that are constantly changing, based on the finicky predilections of social media algorithms. "Pivot to video" becomes shorthand for how talented reporters and editors are made to follow the whims of a management class that increasingly seems in over its head; we, their employees, pivot so many times it seems like we were all just spinning around in circles. I watch as friends and colleagues fall victim to budget cuts and layoffs due to poor business decisions on the parts of leadership, and once again I think of my former Penn classmates, practicing to sound confident about industries about which they knew nothing at all.

"The tragedy of digital media isn't that it's run by ruthless, profiteering guys in ill-fitting suits," writes Megan Greenwell in her last piece for Deadspin in 2019, after the private equity firm Great Hill Partners acquired parent company G/O Media and slashed its staff.* "It's that the people posing as the experts know

---

* Megan Greenwell, "The Adults in the Room," Deadspin, August 23, 2019.

less about how to make money than their employees, to whom they won't listen."

In the 2020s, so-called brilliant businessmen across media (hi, again, Elon Musk!) and entertainment are gutting companies with breathtaking speed. Their ineptitude is particularly astonishing in light of the basic principles that I thought every Marketing 101 student had to understand, concepts like establishing customer trust and building a reliable brand.

In 2023, a variety of outlets begin to use generative artificial intelligence (a supposed cost-saving measure because, presumably, you don't have to pay robots) to supplement their offerings. Each time a publication uses AI to generate sloppy, often factually incorrect articles, it pains me how entirely obvious it is, and how the people at the top don't seem to know or care just how obvious. They seem to expect that readers won't be able to tell the difference, which is both an underestimation and an insult to customers. Especially when, in the successful marketing of journalism far and wide, it is essential for readers to believe that the publication they read is telling them the truth. Formerly respected brands like *Sports Illustrated* and BuzzFeed have become sullied in this manner. Quality, let alone truth, seems once again to be low priority on leadership's list of important product features.

It has been horrifying to witness the devaluation of art by an executive class that cares very little for innovation or creativity or excellence. I always believed that artists and thinkers would find a way to make their voices heard regardless of who was in charge, just as I was once taught that the judicial and the legislative branches of government would serve as checks to executive power.

Now I look at Clarence Thomas, still serving out his life term as a Supreme Court Justice while taking massive bribes from billionaires who collect Nazi memorabilia[*][†] and supporting his wife, Ginni Thomas, who took an active role in trying to overturn the presidential election on January 6, 2021. Add the idea of checks and balances to the list of things I was taught about America that turned out not to be true after all.

———

IN THE FINAL SEASON OF *MAD MEN*, AFTER PEGGY AND JOAN have spent years clawing their way to the middle of their fictional advertising agency (technically at this point Joan is a partner in the firm, but she's still treated like she's at the middle), Sterling Cooper & Partners is bought out by mega advertising corporation McCann Erickson. The women have a meeting with their new McCann Erickson overlords, during which they try to convey the intricacies of the work they've done on their accounts and their plans for the future. But the boys have no intention of listening. "Why aren't you in the brassiere business?" one of the men says to Joan. "You should be in the bra business. You're a work of art."

With controlled rage, Joan and Peggy finish out the meeting, but it never really gets back on track. All of their efforts will be for naught.

Later in the elevator, Peggy attempts to keep it casual. They've kept up appearances so far. "So, should we get lunch?"

<hr>

* Joshua Kaplan, Justin Elliott, and Alex Mierjeski, "Clarence Thomas and the Billionaire," ProPublica, April 7, 2023.
† Jeet Heer, "Clarence Thomas's Rich Friend Collects: Judges, Politicians—& Nazi Memorabilia," The Nation, April 10, 2023.

In response, Joan simply says, "I want to burn this place down."

This scene has become—at least to me—the show's most iconic. I would think of it whenever I was taking stock of my career and felt my ambition flagging—which was often. It's about more than just sexual harassment; it's about how working hard and playing by the rules can be futile and demeaning if the game itself has always been rigged. Peggy and Joan have been on the ground kicking ass, but their new bosses couldn't care less about their hard work.

I watched as various media companies were run into the ground by tech corporations and private equity firms, talented underlings getting laid off at the first sign of financial trouble. Of course, few execs took pay cuts themselves. The people who are making the decisions don't know or care what their employees actually do every day. What good is hard work when it's entirely invisible? How can companies "do well by doing good" when they're, above all other interests, beholden to investors and stockholders who want to see copious returns on investments? Sure, we're no longer in a cultural moment where it's socially acceptable to make comments about coworkers' breasts in meetings, but the fundamental indignities of our work culture are much closer to the *Mad Men* era than HR departments across corporate America would like us to think.

———

I'M STILL A STUDENT IN THAT WHARTON MARKETING 101 course when I first hear the name Monica Lewinsky. She is a little older than me, but she looks like someone I might know. We both shop at the Gap. I'm interested in the headlines about her, even though my official position is that it is None of My Business what the president does in his private life, so long as he manages to lead well.

It's the decade of the erotic thriller, many of which involve teen girls doing the kinds of naughty things that feel more like the fantasies of an aspiring Humbert Humbert than anything that might be considered a viable human impulse. I love them all, storing them on videocassette tapes so I can access them whenever the desire strikes. There's *Poison Ivy* (1992), which stars Drew Barrymore as the nubile title character, who causes havoc for a friend's dad. There's *The Crush* (1993), starring future megastar Alicia Silverstone as a fourteen-year-old temptress who becomes obsessed with an older man and falsely accuses him of rape after he rejects her advances. Consider also *Wild Things* (1998), in which Denise Richards and Neve Campbell play high school students who plot to bring down a teacher, again with a false accusation of rape.

In the '90s, pop culture is full of conniving young women who falsely accuse men of sexual misconduct, as if that were an easy or wise or non-life-ruining thing to do. Even on my beloved *Beverly Hills, 90210*, there is a 1993 episode in which Steve Sanders, the rich frat boy with a heart of gold, is accused of assault by an unhinged actress who can't handle rejection. The episode is set against the backdrop of the Take Back the Night march on the campus of the fictional California University.

Adult women can also be tricky and deceitful, of course. In 1994, author Michael Crichton publishes the reverse gender role novel-turned-film *Disclosure*, in which a spurned former lover who has been promoted to be her ex's boss falsely accuses him of harassing her. Also in 1994, Alan Dershowitz—yes, *that* Alan Dershowitz—publishes a novel called *The Advocate's Devil*, in which a woman who had once been caught lying under oath about workplace misconduct then accuses a basketball star of rape. In retrospect, the plot of the novel actually contains more nuance than I had remembered for an author who has continually argued that the age of consent should be lowered to fifteen years old.

I suppose I heard of Paula Jones in the lead-up to Bill Clinton's first presidential run when I was just a kid. She was someone I could easily dismiss at the time, some crank who was trying to bring down a big man for nefarious reasons. After all, I had seen it happen that way in plenty of movies. Besides, everyone knew that Bill Clinton has always been good for women! His very first executive action in 1993 was to revoke Reagan's gag rule that had banned family planning clinics funded by Title X from presenting abortion as a legitimate option.

Before 1999, I had never heard the name Juanita Broaddrick, who accused Clinton of raping her when she was volunteering for his campaign in the late 1970s in his first run for governor of Arkansas. There were, of course, others: Kathleen Willey, Gennifer Flowers. I had been too distracted by Monica's blue dress to seriously consider all the women who had come before her and the severity of their claims.

A year before I attended that dazzlingly exciting Clinton rally in 1992, I had registered in an ambient way everyone freaking out over the gross jokes Clarence Thomas made to Anita Hill, jokes she later recounted (and recounted again) during his

Supreme Court confirmation hearings. Something about pubic hair and Coke cans. Something about a porn star.

I will think about Hill a lot during Brett Kavanaugh's unbearable 2018 Senate Judiciary Committee hearings upon his nomination to the Supreme Court. He isn't even competent at *acting* like he's not entirely vile, as his predecessors were to different levels. He gives us no material to create an illusion that he is anything more than the kind of overgrown frat boy I experienced in college.

I am grateful to live in a very cozy bubble in which I know very few people who weren't moved by Christine Blasey Ford's testimony, who didn't feel like they were witnessing a great injustice when she was dismissed. But I know that such people are out there, and I know I will encounter them; that's what Twitter is for, after all.

*Well, if you condemn Kavanaugh, you also must condemn Bill Clinton*, some troll on Twitter replies to me when I express dismay.

*Sounds good to me!!!* I reply. I mean it wholeheartedly, and I also know the extra exclamation points will piss him off. Win/win. I have become an equal-opportunity scorner of sex pests of all affiliations, including Axl and Mick and a variety of other actual rock stars as well as former political ones.

I watch these men thrive after having broken the most basic rules of decency, and all I see is entitlement. These are the men who get to feel as if the world is still full of possibility no matter how many times they fuck up, and who get to experience few or no consequences when they do. I have no use for these men or their politics, no matter whom I may have once revered.

# THE SHOW MUST GO ON

Picture me having just turned eleven years old, wearing a black leather miniskirt, a gold lamé blouse, an enormous blond wig, bright red lipstick, and bluish-gray shadow under my right eye, so that I look as though my latest paramour has just given me a shiner. My arm is in a sling. I'm singing my heart out. I'm the happiest I've ever been.

I'm playing Audrey in a junior production of *Little Shop of Horrors* at the JCC. I am committed to the role, having spent hours working on an impeccable New York accent ("Yes, Doctah!"). I am preadolescent but utterly sexed up, playing a brassy downtown girl with a bit of a confidence problem and terrible taste in men, who yearns for the safety and uniformity and predictability of the suburbs.

It's when I'm belting out the ending of "Suddenly Seymour" that I realize who I want to be when I grow up (and I want to grow up as soon as possible): a Broadway star. I begin to collect original Broadway cast recordings on cassette. I study sheet music and have a somewhat impressive collection of half-price Barnes & Noble coffee table books about the magic of Broadway. I listen constantly to a lesser-known Andrew Lloyd Webber musical called *Song and Dance* that's all about the romantic travails of a young woman new to New York City, just like I am going to be one day. I concentrate intently on the coy yet passionate way Bernadette Peters sings every single word, until I have memorized the whole thing, fake British accent and all. I sing the entirety of the show in the shower, to my older brothers' great distress, fantasizing in equal parts about being on Broadway and having a ton of tumultuous love affairs. I am all Pantene and melodrama.

The next year the school musical is *Peter Pan*, and I get the title role. Twelve is a good age to play Peter Pan, that beacon of perpetual youth, that willful dismissal of both responsibility and puberty. A thing I fake when acting in the role of Peter Pan: flying. The intermediate school has neither the budget nor the inclination to pony up for suspension cables and harnesses. Better to just bend at the waist and extend your arms—to suspend nothing but your disbelief.

Another thing I fake when playing Peter Pan: being a little boy. It's easy. Pin my hair back, throw on a green felt costume, under which the only curves of my body are composed of pure baby fat. The role requires an utter lack of sexuality, and for all of last year's aspirational Audrey energy, I am in no position to disoblige. Although I read well above my grade level and have seen a whole bunch of R-rated movies and am already an adult in my mind, my body still refuses to match.

———

THEN ADOLESCENCE COMES FOR ME AT AGE THIRTEEN AND everything changes, but not in the ways I hoped. No newly budding boobs for me. No being taken more seriously by adults. It was all smelly-pitted angst and mood swings and sebum that required scouring with Oxy pads, which stung like a million tiny little wasps in my pores. This was all regular kid stuff that most of my classmates were also enduring, although as always, some of us had an easier time than others.

Puberty beat the shit out of me in unique and astounding ways. My hormones, surging like a two-liter bottle of Diet Coke when you open it immediately after you've dropped it on the floor, caused my blood sugar to rise and fall and rise even higher with seemingly no correspondence to the insulin I was taking or the food I was eating. To spend just about every waking moment preoccupied with how you feel physically is exhausting in a way healthy people can underestimate. When it feels like your body has turned against you, just getting through the day is a challenge.

Every morning my mom or dad would wake me up and first thing we'd test my blood sugar, which back then required squeezing out a big drop of blood from my finger and placing it carefully on a test strip before gently inserting it into a reader and waiting two minutes to get an accurate result. Then I would lie in bed while my mom called my endocrinologist to report the result, so that Dr. Larson could give us instructions on how to proceed: how much insulin I should inject, what I should eat and when.

Then it was off to school. Mornings were mostly fine; I was a little sleepy but alert enough. Then lunch was at 11 a.m., and then by 12:30 or so my body was done. How I dreaded the afternoon, when I knew my body would revolt sometime around geometry class while my classmates went about their days as if nothing had changed.

Inevitably I would find myself sitting in the nurse's office for the umpteenth time, the smell of rubbing alcohol and latex gloves pervading while I rested on a green cot. If I needed a little extra comfort, I'd shake out the army blanket balled up at the bottom of the cot and wrap it around myself. If it was a really bad day, I would wait there for my mom to pick me up and take me home. I had a lot of really bad days.

Physical anguish became mental anguish and then turned back to physical anguish so it was nearly impossible to differentiate, a vicious cycle of pain. The more classes I missed, the more difficult it became to return. My two top recurring nightmares to this very day: that I've tested my blood sugar and my monitor says that it's one million or one billion (all of my monitors have usually topped out at around five hundred), or that I'm in geometry class, having missed approximately one hundred days in a row, and it's quiz time right now and my mind is blank but I have no excuses not to take it.

———

THAT YEAR, THE SCHOOL MUSICAL WAS *ANNIE*. I AUDITIONED to play Miss Hannigan because mentally, I was already an embittered adult with a drinking problem and a sadistic streak. I went to look at the newly posted cast list and when I saw my name next to the title role, it was not entirely a pleasant surprise. It is so rare, in the junior high musical genre, to have to play someone *younger* than you actually are—especially when you believe yourself to be so much more mature than your classmates. It also doesn't help to develop an unrequited crush on the thirteen-year-old boy playing Daddy Warbucks, a confusing incestuous mess.

As much as I felt like an adult onstage, I was also reverting to the very childlike state of needing my mom just about all the time. The immediate relief I felt the moment her car pulled up in front of the nurse's office vanished almost as soon as we walked through the door to the house, terrible guilt trailing behind me, like I hadn't tried hard enough to last through the day. Maybe my teachers and classmates thought I was simply staging an elaborate hoax in order to get to leave school, like I was pulling a Ferris Bueller but with none of the fun.

How difficult it is to require accommodations when you are a rule follower. I always wanted to be at the top of my class, to get all As, to be exemplary, and I was the only one who put pressure on myself. My parents, in fact, were the ones to console me when I was devastated by a less-than-perfect grade, crying over getting a B in seventh-grade science or something else entirely insignificant. And then suddenly my body made it so that being a good student was no longer even close to my main priority.

This is how I know I had a privileged childhood: I was never expected to think about how exhausted and scared my parents were in all of this. I was never made to contemplate their points of view, the havoc that my body was causing in their own lives. Illness makes narcissists of the best of us, I suppose. And I was just a dumb theater kid.

How lucky that I had a mom who was able to leave her job at the Ocean Township Sewerage Authority, where she was a lab technician, to come pick me up whenever I summoned her. That both she and my father had the time and money and flexibility—or *made* the time and money and flexibility—to see to my needs.

By the spring of 1992, right in the midst of *Annie* rehearsals, we had made no headway with my unpredictable blood sugar, and my endocrinologist decided that monitoring me by phone was insufficient. So my parents took a full week off from their regular lives and admitted me to Mount Sinai Hospital in New York City for observation. In my little suburban mind, this was where they treated the hard cases. I had become a hard case. We packed up my books and some clothes and Muffy, the little red heart-holding teddy bear I'd slept with every night since I was diagnosed, and Dad drove us to Manhattan. We listened to *Miss Saigon* or *Jerome Robbins' Broadway* all the way.

For that week we did everything we were told, as we always did. I ate the food that I was given from diet plans made by a nutritionist and nothing more. I took the insulin that I was prescribed right on time. I went with my parents on walks down city streets to get some exercise and fantasize about a time far in the future when I might become a real New Yorker. And yet my blood sugar was as out of control as ever. The doctors shrugged at us and eventually sent me home without much guidance. There would be no easy fix.

Over the next few years, the three of us—me and my parents—went into Manhattan for doctor's visits every couple of months. I can't offer many details about my life during that period of time, or my state of mind. Thank you to my brain for blocking out what I presume are so many unpleasant memories. Good job, brain.

What I do remember, what I will never forget: whenever we saw a doctor in New York we would also, afterward, see a Broadway show. My mom and dad made a little event out of each and every otherwise tedious trip, giving me something to look forward to in the midst of all of this bad fortune.

There was nothing better than to sit in the darkness of a theater and lose myself in someone else's story (yes, that's a *Chess* reference), preferably with lots of singing and dancing. We saw the corny old-timey musicals like *Guys and Dolls* and *Crazy for You*, all optimism and cute costumes and bright colors. We also saw the ones that felt to me like high art: *Les Misérables*, *The Phantom of the Opera*. If they were darker and moodier than the typical Broadway musical, well then so was I!

I identified so much with the two protagonists in *Kiss of the Spider Woman*, the musical adaptation of Manuel Puig's novel about two men confined to an Argentine prison who live in a constant state of fear of torture or worse. But in their cell, these bedraggled, beaten men could let their imaginations run wild, and that's where Chita Rivera came in. She was all color and light and glamour, and I had never seen such an on-the-nose example of what escapism can do for sad people. That dank prison cell was probably less appropriate than the barricades of the pre–French Revolution as a setting for a flashy Broadway musical, and I wanted to live there.

Still, there was joy in going back to the low-stakes cartoon world of *Annie*, with its wholesome delights and happy ending. After so many days out of commission, how exciting it felt to go back to rehearsal, to catch up on all of the floor-scrubbing, dishrag-wielding choreography to "The Hard-Knock Life," to get caught up in an orphan's quest for love and money and a dog of one's own.

There was talk of not allowing me to participate in the show, I later learned, and there were many conversations I wasn't privy to where my parents pleaded with school officials to let me perform. If I couldn't make it through a day of school, said the powers that be, why should I be able to participate in after-school activities?

It was simple logic! My mom and dad never backed down. It was too important for me, for them, to have this one thing that I loved.

I missed approximately fifty-six geometry classes that year, but I made it to opening night of the junior high musical. I was able to don the curly red wig and the mary janes and get up on that stage to sing my heart out.

Everything was supposed to get better eventually; that's what the song "Tomorrow" is all about. I needed to believe in that promise. I needed that sun to come out, and so did my parents.

Unfortunately, no one told the Pomeranian who was cast as Sandy, whom I was supposed to hold in my lap and serenade. I sang to that little dog with all of the hope and conviction I could muster, and Sandy the Pomeranian sneezed wet sneezes in my face for the entirety of the song. This became a kind of worldview: you can try real hard and hit all your notes and still, somehow, find yourself covered in dog snot at the end.

After that terrible year, my body calmed down a lot, and what a gift it was to be able to obsess about my grades once again. And I had learned an important skill: I learned to mask it better when I wasn't feeling great, to "smile when I was low" à la "There's No Business Like Show Business." Literally, though, I really did learn to smile when my blood sugar was low, to keep going even if I felt a little disoriented. I wouldn't let anything stop me. The following year, I had perfect attendance at school and a 4.0 grade point average and the conviction that I would do every single thing I could to never feel out of control again. So yes, the seeds of my OCD were firmly planted at the ripe young age of fourteen.

That year I got to play The Mistress in a community theater production of *Evita*, which meant performing and interacting with real adults and staying out at rehearsals till late at night. On performance nights, I would stand center stage in an old-timey satin slip holding a battered old suitcase, all eyes on me, singing a song about how I'm a hardened teenage sex worker at the end of an affair with a vicious dictator. I was officially back, baby!

Later I would read Barbara Ehrenreich's *Bright Sided*, about her own diagnosis with breast cancer, and how horrified she was to realize that being a "warrior" is the only socially acceptable way to deal with debilitating illness. We want our sick people to inspire us, battle diseases, tough it out when faced with adversity. As Susan Sontag detailed in *Illness as Metaphor*, we constantly use the language of war to talk about physical phenomena over which we have very little control: beat cancer, fight through the pain. Where does that leave those of us who are just too tired?

In 2008, Type 1 diabetes was officially recognized as a disability under the Americans with Disabilities Act. What a paradigm shift, to consider myself disabled rather than just weak or tired or un-lucky. Still, grind culture had already gotten me. I'm finally an adult woman who gets to be in charge of my own body, to make the choices that feel right to me. But prioritizing my health over work still feels mildly transgressive to this day.

Even though I've lived in New York City for twenty years, I don't see many Broadway shows anymore. Have you seen ticket prices? But one night in late 2021, I received comp tickets to a buzzy new play, and Josh and I were prepared to don our N95s and head into Manhattan to see it. First we ate an early dinner at a neighborhood deli, and at the end of that dinner, as happens more often than any of us would like, my blood sugar had become inexplicably low.

There I was, sitting in the deli and realizing that my neighbor's corned beef reuben had become blurry. Josh ordered dessert, a proper dessert, a Nanaimo bar that was chocolatey and crunchy, and I wish I'd been more with it so I could describe it better now. That's what happens when dessert is a lifesaver rather than just a treat.

We could have continued on with our night once my blood sugar had stabilized, hopped on the subway still a little shaky and raced to the theater to make it by curtain time. But I went home instead. I chose to go home, chose to sit on my couch and put my feet up, chose to allow myself to recover in my own time. That choice is a gift. I learned it from my parents.

There is so much to be said for persevering, for embodying that "the show must go on" spirit. But whenever I have doubts I will remember how, at the time in my youth when I experienced a life-shattering lack of control and all of the world wanted me to fight through it, my parents let me rest. I will always be grateful.

# I WANNA BE RICH

It is the year 1985. Or 1986? Put it like this: my mom regularly teases my bangs for me before I get on the school bus every morning.

It is my brothers' birthday. They're twins, five years older than I am. In an absolutely baller move, my parents and I pick them up from Hebrew school in a stretch limo. Imagine us showing up to Temple Beth El in some long-ass Lincoln, complete with sunroof and tinted windows, watching the other kids gawk at the car, eager to determine what incredibly important person could be inside. Then the driver, who in my head looks like Alfred from Batman, steps out and calls my brothers' names.

Imagine having that kind of clout. What celebrities my brothers were, even for one glorious moment!

The limo takes us to one of the Jersey Shore's fanciest restaurants, or at least one as fancy as I've ever seen. Cream-colored cloth napkins folded into fan shapes at each place setting, empty wineglasses placed around the table, tiny little plates to the sides of the main plates, which I'm told will be for the bread that will soon be served. A lavishly appointed chandelier, and out the window behind it, you can see the scum-twinged darkness of the Atlantic Ocean.

It's only when I look around the restaurant and watch the adults sitting at other tables that I realize something is wrong. The other diners are ostensibly being fancy and having sophisticated conversations. But all the while they are dining on—no, slurping down—what appear to be actual monsters. I watch in horror as grown adults, who are for some reason all wearing bibs, pull apart the bodies of terrifying sea creatures, feasting on the meat inside. To this day I do not eat lobster.

In the 1980s, it seemed like everyone wanted to be rich above all else, and I was no exception. Overconsumption was sold to me like a sugary cereal during Saturday-morning cartoons, or the fanciest toy in the Sharper Image catalog, some advanced-looking tchotchke that would make my life increasingly better if my parents would just simply buy me one. *Please.* On TV, *Lifestyles of the Rich and Famous* touted Jacuzzis and waterbeds and mega-yachts, and on my brothers' bedroom walls were center-folds of models on some tropical beach, draping themselves across Ferraris and Lamborghinis. Speaking of water sports, this is also the era that brought us Donald Trump and his gold toilet.

But my revulsion to the shellfish slurpers that day was my very first inkling that there might be something disgusting about accumulating wealth and excess. It would take many more years for me to realize that the hoarding of wealth is a sign of moral depravity, not business acumen. Until then, my conception of the American Dream was that anyone in this country could work hard and acquire a bunch of stuff, and it was the stuff—what kind and how much—that was ultimately a signal of one's worth as a person. Anyone, with enough fortitude and ambition, could become Scrooge McDuck diving into his massive pile of gold coins and jewels.

The wealth gap would have to grow increasingly dire before I would come to believe that in a just world, billionaires like Scrooge wouldn't exist at all.

———

Growing up in the New Jersey suburbs, obsessed with the idea of what it might be like to be a zillionaire, I loved to hear my mom's stories about her great-uncle Barney. Barney lived on Park Avenue in New York City and always traveled by chauffeured limousine. My great-great-uncle opened his eponymous men's clothing store in 1923 at Seventh Avenue and Seventeenth Street in Chelsea, and over the next decades of the twentieth century it would evolve into an iconic department store and worldwide fashion destination.

Barneys was a particular kind of rags-to-riches success story, one that I'll call the Jewish American Dream. You start out selling schmattas and end up the scion of an elite family business that over three generations becomes a cultural institution that even WASPs admire and envy. Barneys was the epitome of the kind of glamour I coveted but could never attain as a young woman. In its heyday, it was, according to *New York Times* fashion critic Vanessa Friedman, "unabashedly elitist, proudly exclusionary—you got it or you didn't, and if you didn't, that was your problem, not theirs—and imbued with an arrogance that, at a certain point, began to chafe."[*]

That relatives of mine could be such utter snobs was a triumph and proof that the American Dream was alive and well. Like a Jewish Pygmalion, Barneys had lost its Yiddishisms and grown into an elegant cultural force. This was assimilation in its most successful form.

———

[*]  Vanessa Friedman, "Of Barneys' Bankruptcy, Pride and the Fall," *New York Times*, August 6, 2019.

Just like me, my Jewish ancestors wanted wealth, lots of it. In my youth I was in three different productions of *Fiddler on the Roof* (I played Shprintze twice, Chava once), so I was very much aware of the tribulations of shtetl life, and also of how unflattering babushkas were, then and now, for girls with chubby cheeks. In the face of persecution, the desire to be rich seemed more than logical. It was about survival, power. Money unburdens you from the tides of history; it gives you agency to do, or not do, as you please. It frees you to "biddy biddy bum" all day long, as post-pubescent Tevyes have sung and still sing on school stages all across the tristate area.

But the Jewish American Dream has a consequence that we don't often talk about. Even in the twentieth century, when the promise of security in America was more attainable than it ever was (and might ever be again—who knows, I'm not an economist), those who were able to lift themselves out of poverty and persecution to a more-than-comfortable life were often still unable to relax and enjoy the spoils. Work becomes an obsession, and the impulse to hoard, so rational in times of deprivation, becomes noxious in times of abundance. And, of course, the second or third generation gets their outsized inheritance without needing to have done any of the work (I'm looking at you, Sackler family). Not a lick of acumen was required. Gold coin pool for all.

———

EARLY IN HIS CAREER, MY GREAT-GREAT-UNCLE WAS KNOWN as the "Cut-Rate Clothing King," which is yet another way I know that paying full retail price isn't in my DNA. Barneys initially made its fortune by selling brand-name men's clothing at heavily discounted prices and focusing on innovative advertising, like a "Calling All Men to Barneys" spot in the style of the *Dick Tracy* radio show. Legend has it that Barney pawned his wife's wedding ring in order to open the store in Chelsea. The store's motto at the time was a pure tribute to his Lower East Side roots: "No bunk, no junk, no imitations."[*]

My great-grandfather, Samuel Pressman, was Barney's brother. When Barney opened the store on Seventeenth Street, Samuel worked there, too. Samuel's Hebrew name was Tomkin Schmuel, so at the store everyone called him Tommy. My mother grew up going from her home in Jersey City to Chelsea to call on her grandfather whenever a man in the family needed a suit. She remembers that as a child, the store seemed much less intimidating than uptown department stores like Saks.

"When I walked into that store," she told me, "I had an enormous sense of pride that my family had started a big business in New York, with my great-uncle's name in big bold letters above the door. I was treated like a little princess by my relatives who worked there and their associates."

In the 1960s, Barney's son Fred started to take the store in an entirely new, decidedly more upscale direction. Fred is credited with bringing Giorgio Armani's tailoring to Americans in the 1970s. He also initiated the opening of a women's store at Barneys, which his son, Gene, is credited with having built into a nexus for luxury and unique fashions. The store where my mom had played

---

[*]  Judy Klemesrud, "Barney's Barney: A 'No-Bunk' Original; Calls With New Ideas," *New York Times*, December 9, 1979.

with the three-way mirrors in the free alterations area was changing quickly. Barneys was about to become bigger than my mom's
side of the family had ever imagined, and then it would become
*too* big.

———

ONE OF MY FAVORITE TROPES, IN CHILDHOOD AND NOW, IS
the shopping spree montage. A glamorous woman is weighed
down with shopping bags from all of the most glamorous stores,
having breezed through and picked out all of the best merchandise, usually to the tune of some empowering pop song. This
woman experiences no dressing room angst at Contempo Casuals
because her legs are too short, her waist too unwieldy to fill out
the form. Her body matches her credit card limit, with propor-
tions inaccessible to the average human. Vivian in *Pretty Woman*
and Cher in *Clueless* were my superheroes.

By the 1980s, Barneys wasn't just lavish in a Wall Street "greed is
good" kind of way; it was also cool. Visionary, really. In 1986, the
same year my whole family made the trip into Manhattan to find
bar mitzvah suits for my older brothers, Simon Doonan was hired
as the window dresser at Barneys, beginning his career of making eccentric, over-the-top creations that made pedestrians stop
and gawk. 1986 was also when upstart models Naomi Campbell,
Christy Turlington, and Linda Evangelista[*] were featured in Barneys ads, and that November, the store hosted Decorated Denim,

---

[*]  Bethany Biron, "The Rise and Fall of Barneys," *Business Insider*, October 31, 2019.

a high-profile auction in which Barneys commissioned artists to modify Levi's denim jackets and sold them to benefit AIDS research. Models included Madonna and Iman wearing denim that had been embellished by Paloma Picasso, Keith Haring, Jean-Michel Basquiat, and Andy Warhol.* The 1980s Barneys still feels like the closest a luxury fashion retailer has gotten to making actual art, or at least coexisting with art in a non-slimy way.

You would think a trip to Barneys would have been thrilling for me, and it was, much later. But for all my childhood fantasies of shopping sprees, especially ones with Madonna's "Material Girl" playing in the background, when I think back to my trips to Great-Great-Uncle Barney's store, I have no memories of such lavishness. Barneys may have been transformed from simple clothing store to cultural phenomenon, but my parents still primarily used Barneys as a place to buy men's suits. My favorite activity at Barneys was squatting on the floor in the men's department to play underneath the hanging suits, letting the dress pants whip my face like they were wipers at a car wash and I was a dirty Buick. We did get a 15-percent-off family discount, but that got us just about nowhere, because 15 percent off increasingly unaffordable clothes was still unaffordable.

I wish I could tell you about Barneys in its glory days, its avant-garde designer clothing and opulent displays, but in truth, my strongest memory of going there as a child has nothing to do with the store or its windows. It's the grilled cheese I'd get at the hole-in-the-wall diner next door, the name of which has been lost

---

* Phillip Picardi, "How ACT UP and the Downtown Fashion Scene Came to the Rescue," *Vogue*, December 16, 2020.

to time. Later, I would read about Fred's, the restaurant named after Barney's son, where all the city's big shots would go to have their power lunches. I'm sure the salade Niçoise (or, god forbid, lobster!) was great, but to me, nothing could be better than that grilled cheese.

———

BARNEYS CONTINUED TO GROW IN CULTURAL CACHET IN THE 1990s. In a November 2019 article in *Vogue*,[*] Steff Yotka writes, "More than just a place to discover Rick Owens leather jackets and Proenza Schouler bustiers, Barneys acted as a connective tissue in the New York creative scene. It was where in-the-know people went to shop . . . more upscale, whimsical, and international." The store carried unique products that patrons from all over the world came to purchase—Barneys was the first American store to carry product lines from Christian Louboutin to Azzedine Alaïa and Yohji Yamamoto, among other designers.

Barney's grandchildren, my very distant cousins whom I have never met, were running the store at the time and adding their own personal touches. In 1993, Gene and Bob Pressman spent approximately $185 million on a new flagship store on Madison Avenue and Sixty-First Street.[†] Just a few years later, the store in Chelsea that I'd visited as a child closed. Meanwhile, the enor-

*   Steff Yotka, "'Barneys Started Our Career': Five New York Designers Remember the Department Store's Impact as Its Fate Hangs in Limbo," *Vogue*, November 1, 2019.
†   Jennifer Steinhauer, "TURMOIL AT BARNEYS: THE DIFFICULTIES; Barneys Is Seeking Bankruptcy, Citing Fight With Partner," *New York Times*, January 12, 1996.

mous expansion (new stores opened everywhere from Houston to Tokyo) weighed on the finances of the privately held company, and the family lost control of Barneys after its first bankruptcy filing in 1996. At the time, I was working part-time at The Gap in Monmouth Mall, using my employee discount to set aside clothes that I would bring to college.

I followed along with the news over the years: in 2004, my distant relatives sold their remaining interest in the company, even as the uptown location was thriving. Still the brand continued to grow and evolve, and Barneys was still a cultural force as we entered the new century. Just consider the generations of TV fashionistas who shopped there over the decades: the cast of *Mad Men*, the ladies of *Sex and the City*, the ladies of *Gossip Girl*.

In 2007, I moved to a five-hundred-square-foot studio apartment in Chelsea, not too far from the original Barneys store. The space had become a Loehmann's, a luxury discount store that suited my needs perfectly. I would spend hours in bad lighting, picking through racks for $40 dresses the same way I imagined other, more elegant women would rummage through cardboard boxes at Barneys's famous warehouse sale to find $800 designer sweaters discounted to $500. I would try on my findings in the shabby Loehmann's communal dressing rooms, where women of all shapes and sizes and backgrounds competed for mirror space, and I would delight in getting a Loehmann's receipt that would show me exactly how much money I'd saved off the retail price. I think I still have one where I saved 85 percent on a Nicole Miller dress. By the time Barneys returned to its old Chelsea space for a short run starting in 2016, I was too busy mourning the loss of Loehmann's to be excited about the homecoming.

As the years went on, Barneys's splendor continued to degrade. Its ownership changed hands several times, from retail corporations to hedge funds, which watered down its identity. According to the *New York Times*,* a 2010 renovation made Barneys look more like its rivals, "as fish tanks and mosaics were swapped out for generic marble." Then the company went bankrupt and was liquidated by a blur of corporations and hedge funds and financial firms, which seems to be the fatal conclusion to a lot of American Dreams these days. Watching Barneys dissolve into a hodgepodge of capital still felt like an enormous personal loss, even though I never could afford to shop there myself.

———

IN AUGUST 2019, BARNEYS FILED FOR BANKRUPTCY FOR THE second time and was sold off for parts. The financial firm B. Riley Financial held a liquidation sale at Barneys† at the end of that year, and what remained of the store was a motley collection of left-overs and *EVERYTHING MUST GO* signs. In January of 2020, the *New York Times* reported that since November, "employees at Barneys's flagship at Madison Avenue have been in limbo, lacking basic information about the store's closing date, severance pay

---

* Vanessa Friedman and Sapna Maheshwari, "Barneys Is Sold for Scrap, Ending an Era," *New York Times*, November 1, 2019.
† Ibid.

and their benefits."* The welfare of the sales force, which used to be revered and well compensated† for its personalization and panache (according to my mom, at least) began to seem like an afterthought.

Saks Fifth Avenue now owns the Barneys brand, which still exists even if the stores do not. In September of 2023, the fast fashion monster Forever 21 announced a partnership with the Barneys brand—a sentence I never thought I'd write. The store that my mother used to find too intimidating as a kid has approved a collaboration for Barneys with a former fixture of malls everywhere. Which is how the institution I'd most aspired to fit into for my whole life became aligned with a fast fashion clothing company that is notorious for consistently ripping off fashion designers of all stripes and using sweatshop labor to do it.

After all this time, I can finally afford to buy stuff from Barneys, but it turns out I no longer want to. Alas, my own Jewish American Dream is a modest one: to live in a city where mom-and-pop stores stick around and workers are treated with dignity. Swimming in a pool of gold coins, after all, is, at the very least, unsanitary and at most, very painful.

---

* Sapna Maheshwari, "Barneys Workers Feel Used as They March Store Toward Death," *New York Times*, January 16, 2020.
† Ibid.

# A SERIES OF UNFORTUNATE SALARIES

I'm marching on a picket line outside the offices of Harper-Collins, the publisher of this very book you're now reading. It's a gray and freezing day in Lower Manhattan, right near Wall Street, and every now and then an errant snowflake lands in my hair so that I feel foolish for not bringing a hat. Still, I carry my bulky sign—*United Auto Workers on Strike!*—and tell myself that if 250 publishing workers can be out on the streets protesting all winter and forfeiting their already meager paychecks, then I, as a supportive author, can tolerate one hour in the cold.

It is December 16, 2022, and HarperCollins employees have been on strike for months now. Their demands are modest—a higher entry-level salary ($50,000 a year rather than $45,000, still peanuts for a job based in Manhattan in 2022) and more diversity in hiring—demands that a publisher owned by one of the world's largest media conglomerates should easily be able to provide. Yet management still refuses to come to the bargaining table. The situation is dire. There seems to be no end in sight, no limit to corporate greed. So why can't I stop smiling?

———

THE YEAR IS 2003, AND I AM WEARING A BRAND-NEW DRESS, some rayon floral number that cost $14.99. I've just bought it off the sale rack at the H&M a block down from the Simon &

Schuster office, after a run-in with a Xerox machine left my original outfit covered in black ink. A little bit of lipstick in the office bathroom, and I'm ready for happy hour.

We meet at our favorite dive bar on the Lower East Side, nursing vodka sodas—two-for-one from 5–8 p.m.!—and digging into the free bowls of nut mix that could count as dinner if you eat every morsel and don't mind having a few stomach issues after. We don't mind. I, for one, have just spent my dinner money on the new dress.

I'm tired and headachy from working under fluorescent lights all day, but I rejoice in having finally regrouped with my people, a bunch of other assistants who also have big ambitions and very small bank balances. That they currently function more like a Greek chorus forecasting doom and sorrow rather than the modern-day Algonquin round table I always imagined is absolutely fine with me. Scintillating dialogue can come later. For now, we'll go around and try to one-up each other with horror stories from work. Note that I've changed names here to protect the innocent—and the underpaid.

"Michelle is trying to avoid an author of hers who is really, really needy," sighs Maddie, a publicity assistant who started on the same day as I did. "So every time he calls I have to tell him she's not available, and when I ask him if I can take a message, he starts telling me his life story." Maddie makes the universal sign of the embattled assistant: elbows on the table, hands rubbing her temples. "Apparently his wife is leaving him, and his cat has a urinary tract infection."

"I walked in on Emily breast-pumping in her office," says Kevin, token male assistant friend. "I was so embarrassed, but I didn't want *her* to feel embarrassed, so I stayed and tried to make conversation?" Poor Kevin, reminding us that men, too, are sometimes susceptible to upspeak. "I don't think she took it that well because she dropped a whole bottle of breast milk on the ground and screamed. I ran out and slammed the door, and I think we've mutually decided to pretend like it never happened."

"This morning, Frank told me to go to the bodega and buy him animal crackers before our 10:30 marketing meeting," Amy started, fluffing up her bangs. "They were out of the regular kind, so I took a risk and bought the chocolate-flavored ones. He screamed at me when I got back. Told me I don't follow directions well." She takes a long swig of her well whiskey and Coke and belches.

"Last night I had to stay at the office until nine, trying to put together photo credits for this enormous history book that's coming out this fall," I say, gulping my drink; already, we've forgotten that we're supposed to be making them last. "I mean, I had no other plans, but the boss lady didn't know that."

We're doing a cute little bit—"Fresh-faced college grads find out that work is hard"—editing out the egg Maddie had to donate in order to pay rent. The fact that Lisa couldn't make it out tonight because she'd had to give up her room in her Brooklyn apartment and is instead commuting ninety minutes on New Jersey Transit to make it back to her parents' house at the end of the workday. There is certainly no mention of Audrey, a quiet yet quick-witted Black woman who lasted one year as an assistant before moving on to get her teaching degree.

I'm just about to make my way to the bar, flashing a $5 bill so the bartender knows I mean business, when I hear Amy say, "This is so not fair. We shouldn't stand for this."

"We should unionize," says Maddie.

I roll my eyes and make a jack-off motion with my hand. I'm so eloquent.

"What are we, longshoremen who want to do some racketeering by the pier?" I scoff.

Simon & Schuster is not the Triangle Shirtwaist Factory, after all. We are not Sally Field, standing on that table in that one movie. We knew what we were getting into when we went into this business, and we did it anyway.

I squeeze some lime into my vodka soda (vitamins!) and feel a little sorry for Maddie, so deluded in her idealism that she thinks this is how the world works. I myself am not so naïve. The labor movement is not meant for aspiring white-collar people like us.

———

VERY FEW PEOPLE GET INTO BOOK PUBLISHING BECAUSE they want to get rich. They do it for the privilege of working around books. When I started out as an editorial assistant in 2001, I knew that I would be subjected to years of dues-paying. I was told again and again that there was no way to learn about the industry without sitting in the middle of it (at the bottom, of course) and observing, by doing secretarial work and watching more experienced editors make all the decisions, with the goal of becoming one of those editors someday. The thrill of knowing that I was on the path to putting wonderful new books into the world was enough to sustain me, and I held out hope that if I can stick it out long enough I might even begin to earn a livable wage.

Over the course of my editorial career, I began to realize that publishing had very little to do with what I liked to read or introducing great literature to a wide audience. Only sometimes was the job about putting books out into the world that I—or anyone at the company—actually believed in. Very few of the books I felt passionately about were likely to garner any significant sales. (These are the art-versus-commerce blues that just about every bright-eyed young go-getter in a creative industry gets to experience.) So instead, I worked on business books and self-help books, diet books and ghostwritten celebrity memoirs, anything that had a fighting chance of hitting the *New York Times* Best Sellers list. I worked on the books that my bosses chose to work on, or books that their bosses chose for *them* to work on. My input on the whole process counted for very little, of course. I was meant to be occupied with other things.

My life as an assistant in the early aughts can be characterized as a constant battle with paper. I sent faxes. I chased down confirmation sheets for those faxes and stuck them into my boss's plastic inbox trays. I filed. I got down on my hands and knees to squeeze stacks of paper into cabinets that were already overflowing with contracts and author photos. I took phone messages. I wrote them on triplicate paper, so my boss could have one copy and I could also keep a record for lord knows why. I opened mail. I shuttled interoffice envelopes from floor to floor. I put proposals sent by literary agents in my boss's inbox and kept unsolicited manuscripts to respond to myself. I photocopied. I made twelve copies of a four-hundred-page manuscript so that everyone on the editorial team could weigh in and ended up with a backache. I tried to clear the jams in the photocopier, but sometimes the

Xerox machine would reject my most earnest attempts at paper management, and I'd have to buy a new dress at H&M. And all these paper cuts, all of this agita, would one day lead to the creation of an actual $24.95 hardcover that people might buy.

In my off hours I read books about the golden era of publishing, memoirs by legendary editors who seemed to have lived like rock stars, all artistry and excess. Older colleagues told me wistfully about the days when they could smoke in their offices, *Mad Men*–style, while their secretaries ran personal errands for them. There were the much-glorified three-martini lunches with brilliant authors, followed by postlunch naps on their office floors, and the freedom to publish whomever and whatever they pleased, with no numbers guy constantly worrying them about the bottom line. Just about everyone who worked in publishing at the time was independently wealthy, so they'd been free to ignore those pesky numbers. Corporations were ruining the book business, with budgets slashed and art being turned so blatantly into commerce. The gentlemen's agreements of the past were being supplanted by legalese and digital marketing teams. To the old guard, this was downright vulgar. I couldn't help but agree.

The industry I inherited was mired in the muck, somewhere between the worst of the so-called good old days, when rich white men ran everything according to their own whims, and the contemporary shift to corporate publishing, in which (mostly) rich white men ran everything according to the whims of their company's executive board and shareholders.

Publishing workers like me were caught in the middle, weighed down by corporate bullshit (less flexibility, more paperwork, always the eye on the bottom line) but still burdened by the elitism of the past. Even by the time my career had begun, the problems of the past still plagued us. The publishing industry screeched to a halt every August as bosses escaped to their vacation homes while assistants were left behind in the city to fret about making rent on a room in an apartment shared with three roommates. Unbridled misogyny still meant that sexual harassment was a rite of passage for generations of assistants. Getting a job in the first place was still about where you went to college or who you knew, which meant that diversity of race and socioeconomic class and educational background was hardly a consideration.

"This is just how it is" is the common refrain of institutions that don't want to even consider change. For most of the early aughts, I sat dutifully in editorial meetings, taking notes and keeping quiet. The rules, spoken and otherwise, said that junior staff were there only to listen, with the hope that the wisdom of their elders would trickle down to them slowly but steadily, like how Reaganomics was supposed to work. Later, in 2014, I worked at a digital start-up where twenty-four-year-olds ran the meetings, and other twenty-four-year-old colleagues expressed their opinions with abandon. The culture shock was disorienting. I couldn't believe that young staffers were being treated like estimable people with valid concerns right away. My years in publishing had trained me to believe that personhood would have to be earned, like a gold star or a promotion, which was more likely just a title change with no raise.

In 2007, I was promoted to associate editor, and I began to think that all my dues-paying might finally pay off. One more promotion, and I wouldn't have to assist a senior editor any longer, would get to work on my own books and maybe even get my own office. Instead, I got laid off when my imprint folded

four months into my new role. I found out the hard way that
the only thing hard work guarantees is unpaid overtime. We were
told to see all the indignities and abuse, making what often aver-
aged out to be less than minimum wage, as a fun challenge, an
experience upon which we'd lovingly look back to feel proud of
how much our skin had thickened, the fact that we'd survived.
We were meant to be satisfied with being told, "That's just how it
is." This was how things in this industry had always worked, they
said, and would continue to work, over and over and over again.
I believed them.

———

WHEN I SOLD THIS BOOK TO AN IMPRINT OF HARPER-
Collins, I knew I would have to do some cognitive acrobatics.
Very few book publishers—even the smallest ones—are entirely
pure. Even self-publishing is almost entirely dependent on Amazon,
the company whose labor practices don't allow for warehouse
workers to take proper bathroom breaks.

But HarperCollins is owned by News Corp and is therefore
particularly noxious, aligned as they are with the Fox News propaganda machine. And so it is that noted book-banner Ron DeSantis
and I share the same publisher.

I'm ashamed to tell you how long it took me to realize that
just because a book is categorized as nonfiction, doesn't mean
it's necessarily true. "Nonfiction" is just a marketing term for a
book in which the author(s) purports to be telling the truth. Fact-
checking, I learned, is the legal and financial responsibility of the
author rather than the publisher (many thanks to Joanna Arcieri,

who fact-checked this book). "The responsibility for the accuracy of the text does rest on the author; we do rely on their expertise or research for accuracy," a spokesperson for Hachette Book Group told *Esquire* in 2020.* Each and every publisher that constitutes the Big Five largest companies in corporate book publishing has a similar policy, one that provides authors only a legal read of soon-to-be-published books (hi to the HarperCollins attorney who reviewed this manuscript) rather than thorough fact-checking. As you might imagine, some authors are more invested in getting the facts right than others, which is why misinformation runs rampant in so many books that purport to be true. My book proposal included this chapter you're reading now, in which I call out HarperCollins in particular for being complicit in the spread of disinformation, but the good people at Ecco bought the book anyway.

Even in my most bright-eyed, head-down days, when I really believed that literature could change the world, there were books that just felt wrong, books that seemed to make the world a little worse simply by existing. Rush Limbaugh's smug face sneered at me from the covers of bestselling hate bombs, while Glenn Beck's "global warming is a hoax" book and Michelle Malkin's anti-immigrant screeds sat on the free shelf right next to Ernest Hemingway and Edith Wharton reissues.

Drilled into me back then was the belief that putting out big bestsellers, no matter the style or substance, would always be a net positive. Any lies that Oprah-endorsed quacks (yes, I did briefly

---

* Emma Copley Eisenberg, "Fact Checking Is the Core of Nonfiction Writing. Why Do So Many Publishers Refuse to Do It?" *Esquire*, August 26, 2020.

work on a Dr. Oz book) presented as research-driven fact were acceptable because the profits from such books might enable me to acquire the kind of fiction I actually liked to read. The homophobic rants of Fox News personalities had a built-in audience, so their guaranteed sales just might allow me to take a chance on a debut story collection from an unknown queer writer. Extremism and hatred and fake science and conspiracy theories sold books, and the spoils of those books would allow new literary voices to emerge.

Publishing a diversity of opinions is paramount, or so my elders in the book publishing industry have repeatedly told me. Even though they are corporate entities, publishers see themselves as arbiters of free speech, fighting the good fight to make sure a variety of voices—both sides, if you will—can be heard. Under this logic they are able to convince themselves that publishing hatemongers and charlatans is downright noble, even if—especially if—their ideas make you uncomfortable. They could not imagine such ideas could ever cause harm greater than their own discomfort. Even at my most naïve, it had always seemed to me that the Founding Fathers never granted anyone the inalienable right to receive big advances and bigger marketing budgets from large publishing conglomerates for their abhorrent opinions, but what did I know?

I didn't really have to reckon with the book publishing world's complicity in spreading hate and lies at the time. Even though I was battling printers during the day and eating bar nuts for dinner, I was still lucky, so lucky that the content of hateful books produced by the industry in which I was complicit didn't directly impact my life. So it was easy to keep focus on the daily drudgery and not big-picture concerns.

Then Trump was elected. Then children were separated from their families at the southern border. Then over a million Americans died in a global pandemic, then Roe v. Wade was overturned, then there was a massive uptick in books being banned in school libraries. I watched the dehumanization of trans people become a right-wing talking point that was then often validated by centrist Democrats. Every single day I would scroll through Twitter and find some new devastating consequence to, among other things, publishers' role in elevating bigots.

At the same time, companies large and small started promising to make structural changes in the wake of the Black Lives Matter movement, and publishers, whose staff tends to be more homogenous than not (in 2019 the book publishing industry was 76 percent white[*]), saw antiracist books become a profitable new trend. I watched from afar as publishers put out statements about equality and announced the creation of DEI committees, taking the smallest first steps in trying to increase diversity among its workers. Publishers even began to imply that they might value the diversity of their employees' *opinions* as much as they have traditionally valued their authors. Imagine! Next thing you know, some twenty-three-year-old is going to walk into an editorial board meeting with well-thought-out criticism and the other people at the table will listen to it!

It's helpful for me to think of the choice to publish people who encourage the marginalization of others as an issue of

---

[*] Lee & Low Books with coauthors Laura M. Jiménez, PhD, and Betsy Beckert, "Where Is the Diversity in Publishing: The 2019 Diversity Baseline Survey Results," Lee & Low Books, January 28, 2020.

workers' rights rather than freedom of speech. I'm no constitu-
tional scholar, but I know that the people who actually make the
book, who do battle with paper (there's less paper now, but still),
should have a say in what books they work on. Making a barely
livable salary while clearing Xerox jams to get out the message of
one's oppressors is a step too far.

So I cheered when underpaid employees protested Simon &
Schuster's signing of notorious homophobe Mike Pence for a two-
book deal for at least $3 million in 2021. And I signed an open
letter in support of Penguin Random House employees in 2022,
when an imprint of PRH gave Supreme Court Justice Amy Coney
Barrett a whopping $2 million book deal to write a memoir just
as she'd been critical in the overturning of Roe v. Wade. There are
many other examples I won't go into now, other than to say that it
gives me hope every time employees come together to speak out.
Such collective action might not work every time (it didn't, in the
latter two cases), but it is so much more than I could ever have
envisioned in the days when I was charging groceries on my credit
card and shuttling paper around my office. Everyone should have
a union, and that includes publishing workers.

———

THERE'S ONE THING ABOUT HARPERCOLLINS THAT PUTS IT
a step above all the rest of the Big Five publishers: it is, currently,
the only one that has a union. The workers at HarperCollins
have been unionized for decades, and for the past thirty years
have been Local 2110 of the United Auto Workers (turns out the
UAW organizes way more than the auto industry; Local 2110's

initiative to organize white-collar workers has resulted in its representation of a variety of cultural institutions from the Whitney Museum to Film at Lincoln Center*). When I myself was still a wrung-out assistant, a peon of the publishing industry, I knew the HarperCollins union existed, but I couldn't imagine all the possibilities it represented. But in the days post-Covid-lockdown, while I was beginning to work on this very book, I started to hear grumblings. Social media amplified them, turned them into a roar. The labor movement had gotten a much-needed refresh in 2021, with workers from a vast array of fields beginning to organize, from retail workers to instructors at colleges across the country. Kim Kelly, author of *Fight Like Hell: The Untold History of American Labor*, remarked on the sea change in a 2022 interview with *Vogue*.[†] "We saw and are continuing to see," said Kelly, "workers at Amazon and Starbucks—these incredibly well-known corporations that I think a lot of people have accepted as being part of the fabric of their daily lives—go up against the bosses and say, 'We need more from you, because you are literally hanging out in space while we're trying to pay our rent.'"

All across the book industry, people watched as the staff at various other media companies and magazines unionized, analogous creative industries that had similarly treated employees like they should feel lucky just to be there. Creative types were not so different from the baristas and warehouse workers in their desire to be treated fairly. Solidarity across all industries, among all types of

---

* Hamilton Nolan, "The Roots of Today's White Collar Union Wave Are Deeper Than You Think," In These Times, June 17, 2021.
† Emma Specter, "Writer Kim Kelly's New Book, *Fight Like Hell*, Is a Timely Ode to the Labor Movement," *Vogue*, April 28, 2022.

workers, began to feel like the only way to get a better deal for all. We were on the same team.

Then, for the first time in ages, the union at HarperCollins began bargaining for a better contract. Even better, many Harper-Collins employees who were too high-level to join the union also vocally supported the effort. (But not all; I'm a petty bitch, so I absolutely took note of all the scuttlebutt about holdouts.) It took many more years than I'd like to admit before I realized that if publishing is simply a corporate business, and profit its main goal, then all employees of the company should earn a living wage. I know, revolutionary! But for too long I didn't understand that I was a worker, not just a kid with big dreams who was lucky to be there in the first place. That treating workers with basic dignity is good for everyone at the company. Such support was echoed in wide-ranging media coverage that highlighted the union's very modest demands. I knew the workers at HarperCollins had hit a nerve when people outside the book business began to ask me about the strike.

So here I am now, a HarperCollins author, demonstrating solidarity with the workers agitating for change. I'm one of many stomping along the sidewalk in a long and narrow oval outside the publisher's office, mid-December mixed precipitation plunking down on us. I enjoy watching the handmade signs go by. *Passion Doesn't Pay the Bills*, one says, and *If Black Lives Really Mattered They'd Pay Us a Living Wage*. Then there are the more whimsical but still righteously angry book-themed signs, which I particularly admire: *Where the Wild Things Are Underpaid* and *A Series of Unfortunate Salaries*.

Twenty years after I myself was a peon of the publishing industry, I am able to access the anger I'd felt back then and use it, I hope, for good. Better late than never. Chants of "What do we want? A CONTRACT! When do we want it? NOW!" feel like music to my ears, and when I get home, my voice will be as creaky as that one time when I went to private room karaoke with a few friends for five whole hours after a messy breakup. Catharsis!

It's galvanizing to realize that I'm standing in a crowd of people who are energized and ready to say that conditions that I thought were entrenched and unchangeable are actually unacceptable. These workers believe that change *can* happen, and that it *should* happen; "this is just how it is" is no longer acceptable. Books matter, yes. Now more than ever. But book *workers* matter, too.

By the time the strike ends, sixty-six days after it first began, HarperCollins will agree to move the starting salary of $45,000 to $47,500, with $50,000 becoming the base by 2025. Such gains might feel meager after a fight so long and messy, but around the same time, the other Big Five publishers will also increase their threshold for entry-level salaries. This feels like a solid victory in a battle that I never even thought could be waged. Still, there is so much more work to do. There will likely still be many naïve little ambition monsters like myself who arrive at an office and are stripped of many of their illusions about what work is, but I still maintain a ray of hope that some cycles can be broken.

There are certain things that we just shouldn't tolerate anymore.

# I FOUND MY LIFE PARTNER (AND MY HEALTH INSURANCE) BECAUSE I GOT LUCKY

'm crying again. It was to be expected. I'm twenty-five minutes into a call with the customer service department for
my insurance-mandated mail-order prescription service, a
Kafkaesque phrase if ever there was one. I began the call speaking in a calm hushed voice, explaining how I'm still waiting
on the delivery of a medicine that, while not necessary for my
everyday survival the way insulin is, is still rather unpleasant to
be without.

But now I'm becoming frantic. I have a work call in fifteen
minutes that I need to prepare for, and my dog, who always seems
to know the most inopportune time to beg for snacks, has begun
to whine at my feet. I apologize for my agitation to the man on
the other end of the line, who's trying his best to help in whatever
capacity he can (not very much). It's not his fault.

Approximately twenty breathing-through-the-nostrils-and-out-
of-the-mouths later, I'm transferred to a different representative
who explains that the company somehow forgot to fill my prescription, but they can have it expedited and get it to me by Friday
(it's Monday). "Is that the best you can do?" I ask, as if we're nego-
tiating the price of a used car. I have one day of meds left.

It's when I hear the follow-up recording from my prescription
provider that I am (once again) struck, punched in the face, by
how broken the American healthcare system is. A cheerful voice

asks, "Would you like to speak to a registered nurse about how to manage without your medication while you wait for delivery?"

I am lucky, I remind myself. This is what luck looks like. I am lucky to have health insurance at all.

———

I HAVE A STORY I LIKE TO TELL ABOUT MY MARRIAGE. NOT about the first night we met (the dive bar in SoHo, the mutual friend, the whiskey, the whiskey, the whiskey); this is not a love story, or at least, not only. It's a story about luck. I found love because I got lucky. I found him, he found me; I wanted him, he wanted me, flaws and all. No work was required on my part. I didn't arrive at some place of spiritual enlightenment, after which I announced to the world, "I am ready for love," with my arms outstretched in the air. My before and after photos look almost identical, except in the after, I'm not alone. I found love because I got lucky. That's it.

We got married. My husband was a member of a union with great benefits, and I was trying to make it in two fields (books, media) that were slowly and then very quickly falling apart. So while floating from one job to another, I went on his health insurance. This made my life better, more stable, in so many ways. I was still lucky, luckier even. Not only had I found love, I had also found health insurance.

What a profoundly fucked up—and profoundly American—thing to say: I found health insurance because I got lucky.

Before I met Josh, it was important for me to believe, to *prove*, that I could take care of myself. I started my publishing career on my twenty-second birthday, and it was a given that I'd always work jobs that offered health insurance. I had a chronic illness that required constant access to lifesaving medications; I couldn't afford to be without benefits. For me, there would be no bartending while finding myself, no rebellion against conformity as if I were a character in a '90s movie who takes a drag of a Parliament Light before saying, "Fuck the man!" or "I could never work in an office."

No, I would be entrenched in corporate culture from day one. There would be abusive bosses but also free soda; the constant underlying threat of layoffs and no overtime pay but also company-sponsored yoga in the conference room. And medical benefits. As long as I worked a full-time office job, there would be health insurance, and that trumped all else. It would never have occurred to me that healthcare was a basic human right that should be easily accessible to all, regardless of employment status.

At that time, I didn't believe in luck (to this day, I have still never bought a lottery ticket); I believed in hard work, like any proud American who has been indoctrinated by the idea of rugged individualism, when really, they were just born lucky. I was a big believer in personal agency, proud to be vigilant about my career and my health. I would not acknowledge the infinite variables in life that were not in my control. I needed to believe there was a plan, and I needed to believe that if I followed that plan, I would be safe. That if I worked hard enough, I could advance from support staff to management, as if I were unlocking new levels in a video game, leapfrogging my way to the middle, if not the top. And this worked for a while, throughout my twenties—but just barely.

By the time I met Josh, I was thirty-five and felt ancient, the way we always seem to feel ancient at whatever age we happen to be. I had been laid off from a publishing job in my late twenties, when my small division was sold to a different company. I had felt the soul-crushing angst of filling out COBRA paperwork (this was pre-Obamacare) and tremendous guilt when I couldn't find another job immediately. I had not only lost my job, but my identity and my seemingly straightforward career path.

Between 2008 and 2017, I worked at a number of book-adjacent start-ups where job security was not guaranteed. In those years I survived multiple rounds of layoffs at three different companies. I'd eaten the free pizza that one internet start-up provided to still-employed staff after each mass firing, so lucky to still have a job at a company so mismanaged, with executives so overpaid, that our colleagues became expendable. I'd seen too many brilliant, industrious people sent flailing for no fault of their own to ever again believe that one could control one's professional destiny. Diligence and determination didn't do shit.

———

IF HARD WORK WASN'T ENOUGH TO BE SUCCESSFUL IN MY career, then why would I ever want to apply the same philosophy in looking for love? I think about all the dating advice I'd received throughout my twenties and early thirties as a single cis woman who, despite attempts at misandrist posturing ("All men are dick-faces," I'd say, swigging from a bottle of Heineken with my best Janeane Garofalo sneer), very much wanted to find a life partner.

There is a certain brand of trolling that single women are particularly subjected to, concern disguised as friendly advice that implies you are simply not trying hard enough when it comes to finding love. As if a strong work ethic is all you need to overcome the smorgasbord of doofs you find on the dating apps. Platitudes came at me from every direction, and each one was insulting in its own special way.

"You have to be less picky," said my mom's friend, as if I were choosing a small appliance or a pair of glasses and not someone whom I hoped to be compatible with for the rest of my life.

"You just need to find a nice guy," said another one of my mom's friends, as if "nice" were not the bare-minimum baseline for any human being I would choose to interact with. Like, no kidding, I should date a nice guy? I should also date a guy who breathes air and smiles sometimes, who knows how to do laundry and bathes regularly.

"You have to put yourself out there," said a coworker, implying that I was being lazy, which, as you know by now, is the insult that stings the most. I will be damned if you think I am anything but a very hard worker!

"You've just got to date like it's your job," said a married friend who'd met her spouse online. Never mind that I was already overwhelmed with my actual job; still I was expected to multitask. This was circa 2008. "Burnout" was not yet a buzzword.

"You can't love anyone else until you learn to love yourself first," said every women's magazine I've ever read, and later, Ru-Paul. As if I had to spend months or years working on all of my shit before I could subject another person to my messiness. I need to fast-forward here and remind you that I am now very happily married, and I still don't love myself all that much. Both things are true at once. Women really can have it all!

When I met Josh and we easily and effortlessly fell in love, I was so relieved (and a little smug) to realize that none of this advice was at all useful. Capitalism emphasizes personal responsibility in all matters, but finding love is a roll of the dice (not that I would ever gamble). It's out of our hands. You can't girlboss your way into love.

That health insurance is tied to finding love is just as cruel and absurd as tying it to your profession. A hard-won lesson that took me longer to learn than I'd like to admit: there are so many things we can't control no matter how hard we might try. No one's health should suffer for that. Imagine if all the morsels of advice that were flung at me as a single woman applied to not only the mysteries of human connection, but access to basic human necessities. It really changes the tenor of the discourse, doesn't it? Dating like it's your job, just so you can get that prescription filled. Learning to love yourself, so you can see that specialist. Wearing a date-night top that is the perfect blend of sexy and sophisticated, so you can get that MRI. These feel like terrible pitches for dystopian reality shows (back, off TLC!) rather than sound strategies for taking care of one's health and well-being. Although I suppose living with a chronic illness in America has always been something of a dystopian reality show.

———

In our wedding vows, I described all the ways that my husband is not "nice." He is generous with his time and money, he is warm, he is compassionate, he is fun, he is sexy as hell—but he is also not nice, just the right amount of not nice, when the situation calls for it. "Your enemies are my enemies," Josh said to me in *his* vows, and I had never felt quite so happy or so seen.

In 2017, we got married on our terms: no obeying the husband, no white dress, no bouquet, no rabbi, no wedding party. Just a lot of joy and food and dancing with loved ones (a huge group slow dance to "Purple Rain" closed out the night perfectly). And, of course, as a woman with an established career and my own sense of self, I didn't even consider taking my husband's last name.

Our lives didn't change all that much afterward, but there was one perk of the institution of marriage that made a difference. For the first time in my adult life, I was able to ditch the corporate world and become a freelancer, exhilarated by the idea of having more time to read and write and think. This was freedom.

And then I received my health insurance card in the mail. At first, I didn't know that it had arrived, because it was addressed to my husband. His name was also on the card itself. Mine was not. When I eventually called the insurance company for one reason or another (an experience as familiar to anyone with Type 1 diabetes as getting out of bed in the morning), a kind customer support representative couldn't find me in the system. Apparently I didn't exist, not until I was able to give them my husband's social security number, which Josh dictated to me and I dutifully relayed.

How could I enjoy my newfound freedom when my identity was virtually erased from the management of my disease? Being an "independent" married woman was starting to feel disempowering in unexpected ways. My name had been replaced by my husband's, quite literally. I'm officially Josh's "dependent," which goes against everything I'd ever strived to be. Had I done feminism wrong?

So now I begin the process of revising my definition of what it means to be empowered: relinquishing some small amount of my control to my husband and trusting that he's on my team, accepting that leaning on other people—even a man!—is not a sign of failure. That being able to come to Josh for comfort after I've had a frustrating call with our health insurance provider is, in fact, lucky. Lucky as hell.

# MY DUMB OBSESSIONS

"It can be really exasperating to look back at your past. What's the matter with you? I want to ask her, my younger self, shaking her shoulder. If I did that, she would probably cry. Maybe I would cry, too."

—Elif Batuman, *The Idiot*

"There are very few human beings who receive the truth, complete and staggering, by instant illumination. Most of them acquire it fragment by fragment, on a small scale, by successive developments, cellularly, like a laborious mosaic."

—Anaïs Nin, *The Diary of Anais Nin Volume 3*

I blame it all on the Miami Sound Machine. It's the summer of 1986, and "The Words Get in the Way" is playing in heavy rotation on Power 95. Gloria Estefan sings about being unable to articulate her complicated feelings for the man who's leaving her, and I am equally unable to say why this adult contemporary pop song affects me so much. I am only seven years old. I tape the song off the radio and, sprawled on my bedroom carpet, I put my ears up close to my boom box and transcribe the lyrics onto a little red notepad. "I don't believe she knows you like I do," I write. "Your temperamental moody side / The one you always tried to hide from me." Surely I have no grasp of what those words actually mean, but it doesn't matter. I still relate. I want to take Gloria's pain and make it mine.

Overwrought ballads bring me so much happiness. I fast-forward through Tiffany's "I Think We're Alone Now" so I can get straight to "Could've Been," the torchiest song ever sung by a girl who performed for tweens in America's malls. When I'm nine, I invoke my other favorite mall maven. I have just hastily broken up with my ten-year-old boyfriend, and I decide to top my original impulsive decision with another, more elaborate one: I bring my beloved boom box to school. During recess I tell my puzzled ex to listen closely to the song I've selected to blast from the speakers, Debbie Gibson's "Foolish Beat": "I could never love again the way I loved you." I pull this stunt a whole year before *Say Anything* comes out in theaters and John Cusack normalizes creepy boom box wielding as an acceptable romantic gesture; I'm a trendsetter. Alas, Eric is too busy playing on the jungle gym to pay much attention to the song lyrics. Our relationship may be done, but I'm just getting started.

I love this small taste of what a tumultuous love life might feel like. From then on, I aspire to be the star of my own breakup cliché montage: to sit on a couch in filthy pajamas surrounded by empty ice cream tubs and snot-filled tissues and whiskey bottles. To cry with abandon on the street and have screaming matches on the phone with a man who evoked too much passion in me to be reasonable. To forsake bathing entirely and to fling myself around dramatically, too overwhelmed by emotion to bother with cleanliness or balance. Having romantic drama, I think, might make me feel like I'm the main character of my own life.

Until I can find The One (whom I will very happily fight with and cry at all the time), I will spend my time looking, plotting, with the hope that one of my crushes might reciprocate enough so we can be obsessed with each other in an unhealthy way that takes over my life entirely.

In college I have a crisis that involves fingering. To anyone who wasn't around in the late 1990s, the previous sentence might sound shocking, but "fingering" was just the name of a program in Telnet that told you which computer your crush was using, and in which building on campus, simply by typing "finger" along with their university email address. Glorious! I finger a wide and diverse array of my classmates, but I favor a few in particular. Multiple times a day I check in on them, feeling a tickle of frisson if they are anywhere nearby.

But then I learn that some enterprising engineering students have invented a program for "reverse fingering," and I stop abruptly. I suggest you take my word on what the term means, because Googling will take you on an entirely different journey: every single person whom I'd ever fingered knew that I had fingered them, and how voraciously I had fingered them. I must have also been able to see who had fingered me, but it's only the shame that still lingers.

As mortifying as the Infamous Reverse Fingering Incident of '98 is, I still go about ranking my crushes, fantasizing about them, my body releasing all kinds of hormones when I pass them on the street. I go to the library in the evening, get a carrel, and instead of opening a textbook, I make lists of Top 5 or Top 10 Crushes and play elaborate games of Would You Rather with myself. At midnight, the rest of the library closes and only the bottom floor remains open for late-night studiers who trickle downstairs carrying overstuffed Jansports and lukewarm large coffees. There, consolidated into one big group, most of us would use the pretense of studying to check one another out. On a good night, my number one and number two infatuations would be "studying" nearby. An irony: I manage to get As in almost all of my classes even though, despite all my hard work, I uniformly fail to make an impression on any of my crushes.

———

"My poor body. My precious body. How had I let her be treated this way? My body was me. To hate my own body was to suffer from an autoimmune disease of the mind."

—Melissa Febos, *Girlhood*

In the years before college, I spend an inordinate amount of time running around a track going nowhere. Riding a bike and going nowhere. Climbing up stairs and going nowhere. I rust out the StairMaster in my parents' basement while watching *General Hospital*. My reward is a raspberry-and-cream-flavored fat free Häagen-Dazs pop. In 2022, I would read reporter Heather Radke's cultural history of the rear end, aptly titled *Butts*, and I would see my teenage self in the author's depiction of why she so desperately wanted to attain Buns of Steel, the name of a popular workout video at the time: "I regularly told myself the incantations at the heart of the neoliberal myth of exercise: that I lacked discipline, that I was lazy, that my life would be better if I were thinner."*

Nothing is scarier to me than the idea of people perceiving me as lazy, even though literally no one except my internal straw man

---

* Heather Radke, *Butts: A Backstory* (New York: Avid Reader Press), 2022, 159.

is saying that I am. When I'm sixteen years old and I hate the way I look, I buy into the bootstraps theory of diet and exercise. I truly believe I can transcend my genetics if only I try hard enough. I'm so good at trying. And with a perfect body, I would be able to transcend all my other concerns. A fail-proof plan.

The 1990s is a particularly easy time to have an obsession with one's body, that decade when even perfectly proportioned super-models are too fat to pull off the look of the moment. Heroin chic is in, and looking as though you eat enough and get a good night's sleep and care about your health is passé.

It is also the era of the food pyramid, a shorthand for government-approved restrictive dieting that works under the assumption that any kind of fat is inherently bad—bad for the body, and bad morally for anyone who wants to take care of their body. For so long, we'd lived in a culture where fat was the enemy, but never before had we received a USDA-sanctioned chart to put on our fridges that laid it out so clearly. Consuming fat is bad, almost as bad as *being* fat.

I study all of the so-called health magazines as if they are text-books, taking dieting tips from publications like *Self* and *Men's Health*, only learning much later, upon listening to the podcast *Maintenance Phase* (tagline: "Debunking the junk science behind health fads, wellness scams, and nonsensical nutrition advice"), that so many of the studies cited in such diet stories were at best inconclusive, at worst had been funded by a company that stood to gain from particular findings.

Meanwhile, my mother, always willing to do the hard work involved to make my life as carefree as possible, fills our kitchen with a cornucopia of fat-free products: American cheese, skim milk, SnackWell's, Entenmann's low-fat pound cake, BBQ-flavored Baked Lay's potato chips.

Dinner is fruit salad, plain pasta with vegetables, a fat-free roll with fat-free margarine to flavor it, and a big salad, no dressing. Dessert is no-sugar-added, fat-free TCBY in exotic flavors like Dutch apple or white chocolate macadamia nut. Later my mom mail-orders these special no-sugar-added fat-free cake slices that I can microwave for a few seconds to try to make them a little bit moist, slap a dollop of fat-free Cool Whip on top, and then ritually eat while we watch *Melrose Place*. Cool Whip still tastes like love to me.

What I didn't know at the time was that my mostly fat-free diet was hell on my blood sugar, requiring at least an hour of cardio everyday to counteract all the simple carbs I was consuming. So exercise became paramount to me, both for diabetes management and for looking hot. I couldn't wait until school was over so I could change my clothes in the bathroom and run to the gym, feeling relief only once I'd started to sweat. And there was tremendous guilt I felt anytime I had to skip my usual workout. A delightful intersection of regular diabetes issues and teenage girl food issues! How fun.

I'm so mad that I still remember this moment, but I do: It's my senior prom after-party, a school-sponsored event to prevent students from running off after prom to get bombed at the beach. So instead we have a magician and dancing and other age-appropriate shit, and then they serve pizza at midnight. Reader, what I most prominently remember about prom is that I ate pizza with real cheese for the first time in years. I had missed it so much, and it was so delicious, but it's all I can think about for the rest of the evening, and here I am describing it to you twenty-five years later. To consume pizza like a normal person and still have room in my head to think about anything else at all would be progress. How could I get there?

There's some relief by the time I get to college in the late 1990s because the nutritional experts and overlords have gone in an entirely different direction. By then, carbs are officially out: fruit is a crime, and bread is even worse. Eating pizza is now bad for *crust* reasons, not *cheese* reasons. But at least I can skip a day on the treadmill every now and then and my blood sugar wouldn't suffer for it as much.

> "She was in love with the idea of intelligence, and she overestimated her own."
>
> —Mary Gaitskill, *Bad Behavior*

I don't sign up for any women's studies courses in college because, I figure, I'm just as good as all my male classmates. I don't need separate classes to explore how we're different, or how we're treated differently. We aren't treated differently! It's the late 1990s, and we are living in the glory of postfeminism. There is no work left to do.

In short, I know absolutely nothing.

Even in college I still tend to get most of my information from magazines, from broadcast TV, from the canon of literature I read in my English classes, and from late-night drunken conversations with other dumbasses who think they know it all. Which is why my world bursts open when my roommate hands me a copy of Naomi Wolf's debut work of cultural criticism. *The Beauty Myth* remains one of the most formative books in my life, and I'm grateful to have read it when I did because it made me question my surroundings in a way that no other book had done.

It felt revolutionary for me to lie in my extra-long twin bed and consider that my disordered eating and my exercise addiction and my constant feelings of inadequacy about my physical appearance were holding me back in ways I hadn't even considered. My good grades and my ambitions had done nothing to shield me from the torment I felt when I looked in the mirror. I was basic. I was exhausted. I was angry. Wolf articulated the feeling that roiled in my belly alongside that unfulfilling banquet of fat-free foods: "Dieting is the most potent political sedative in women's history; a quietly mad population is a tractable one," she wrote.[*]

If Wolf's book felt trite and inadequately argued to anyone paying attention ("Even by the standards of pop cultural feminist studies, *The Beauty Myth* is a mess, but that doesn't mean it's wrong," wrote Caryn James in a 1991 *New York Times* review[†]), then I decidedly hadn't been. I felt empowered. Even Wolf's later descent from shoddy researcher to full-blown right-wing conspiracy theorist (in 2021 she was suspended from Twitter for spreading anti-vaccination propaganda)[‡] hasn't lessened the importance of her early work for me, because *The Beauty Myth* opened me up to a new way of thinking.

So here I am, smug that I'm on the road to releasing myself of

---

[*]  Naomi Wolf, *The Beauty Myth: How Images of Beauty Are Used Against Women* (New York: William Morrow, 1991), 187.
[†]  Caryn James, "Critic's Notebook; Feminine Beauty as a Masculine Plot," *New York Times*, May 7, 1991.
[‡]  David Connett, "Naomi Wolf banned from Twitter for spreading vaccine myths," *Guardian*, June 5, 2021.

oppressive body issues, freed from diet culture in my brain if not my body. It's my first taste of how a simple book might begin to liberate me from the fragilest chains of the patriarchy. I have so much more reading to do.

> "Unrequited love—plain desperate aboveboard boy-chasing—turned you into a salesperson, and what you were selling was something he didn't want, couldn't use, would never miss."
>
> —Elizabeth McCracken, *The Giant's House*

More than anything, I want to be worthy of love under my new semi-non-body-hating paradigm. I trade fixating on food for fixating on boys, focusing less on the diet and exercise section of my favorite women's magazines and going straight to quizzes with titles like "Who Is Your Real Soulmate?" and "Is He Boyfriend Material?" I live out my young adulthood as if I'm a character in one of the Jane Austen novels I read in my Nineteenth-Century British Lit seminar, deep in my own personal marriage plot. And just as Austen's eligible young ladies could divert their attention from all of the political and economic upheavals that took place in the background of her novels, so could I blithely go about my personal dramas without bothering to stop and look around at the wider world.

If love proved elusive, then heartache, at least, is easily accessible as always. Someone doesn't like me as much as I like them, and suddenly I'm engulfed in all-encompassing, wonderful turmoil. It requires special skill to take any minor rejection and turn it into a Greek tragedy, but I have always been gifted and talented.

I have entire mixtapes devoted to some dude I went on two dates with and who then never called me again, delighted to equate my own insignificant dilemma with the big feelings of Fiona Apple and Liz Phair. At the college bar karaoke night I'd sing a ballad—"Angel of the Morning" is a favorite—that's meant for one oblivious patron in the crowd who would absolutely not get the subtext. I'm concocting a whole psychodrama, and he probably won't even get the *main* text, too busy chatting with his friends or ordering another beer, or worse, hitting on someone else entirely. Later, in the grand tradition of angsty white women who find solace in books, I would see myself in Sylvia Plath's journals: "There is so much hurt in this game of searching for a mate, of testing, trying. And you realize suddenly that you forgot it was a game, and turn away in tears."

No one cares what happens in the marriage plot novel after the happy ending. Once the obstacles are overcome and the declarations of love have been made, the heroine is presumed to live out a life in blissful quietude. I prefer contemporary novels that don't resolve with a great big bow at the end. Show me the messy, the *weird*, the uglier the better.

Which is why I'm terribly sorry to report that after I met Josh, my life got better in myriad ways, but one way in particular: I was no longer weighed down by romantic dramas. How silly I felt for wasting so much time when I had been lucky enough all along to have the time and resources to do and to learn, to read and to see. What a deeply unserious, entitled, *feminine* way to be oppressed, to have the means and energy to do great things but to waste so many chances I'd been given.

I want to tell you that I've spent the rest of my life learning and doing and seeing beyond myself. But even though I was no longer doing close readings of every potentially amorous text and DM, using the skills I'd picked up in Nineteenth-Century British Lit, I found new ways to be very much preoccupied with . . . myself. I filled much extra room in my brain with more garbage: antiaging creams, how many gray hairs is too many to have on my head, on my eyebrows. Hair density serums, that one expensive exfoliant that everyone swears really makes them look younger.

> "Ideas come to us as the successors to griefs, and griefs, at the moment when they change into ideas, lose some part of their power to injure the heart."
>
> —Deborah Levy, *The Cost of Living: A Working Autobiography*

I'm as self-hating as ever, but happily married for five years by the time I interview Elif Batuman for my literary podcast in 2022. I loved her previous novel, *The Idiot*, partly because its heroine, her mind equal parts brilliance and utter stupidity, made me feel seen. Selin was also a college freshman in the late '90s who had a terrible fingering problem, and you can bet that when Elif and I were in conversation at Books Are Magic in Brooklyn in 2018 when the paperback of *The Idiot* was published we spent some time reminiscing about the short era when email location was physically traceable.

*Either/Or* is a sequel to *The Idiot* that finds Selin in her sophomore year, still fingering away, horny as ever but more likely to do something about it this time (there is plenty of deeply unsensual sex in the sequel). But in the first pages, she's still very much consumed by Ivan, the object of her obsession in the first book.

"What we call love is so specific. We have this idea that it's natural, it's the birds and the bees," Elif says when I mention how being consumed with the idea of someone can feel a lot like love at that age. "I just remember how lost I felt, how much I wanted and needed and I had no idea how to get it. And love becomes this very appealing filter to see things through, or bucket to put things in. I don't even know which reductive metaphor to use." She laughs. "It becomes a kind of ideology."

Imagine me, still woefully under-read in feminist theory to this day, having this conversation about a novel and getting as close to having a cartoon light bulb turn on in a little bubble above my head as I ever had. "Part of what I wanted to do in the sequel to *The Idiot* was unpack how I arrived at all of the different assumptions I'd made," Elif tells me. "I was thinking of how much of behavior we think of as being natural or as universal is actually some super specific thing that some guy made up for some reason, which is a really political realization."

In her research for *Either/Or*, Elif told me she read the works of second-wave feminists that she'd never gotten around to, going back to rethink a lot of the assumptions she had made about sexuality as a young woman.

"Shulamith Firestone talks about romance and love as a way that women are depoliticized," Elif tells me, referring to Firestone's work *The Dialectic of Sex: The Case for Feminist Revolution*. "It's something that wastes their time and keeps them out of the political sphere and tied up with problems that are private and thus not political.

"That's another thing I wanted to explore in *Either/Or*," she explains, "the way these girls' thoughts are subsumed with these guys who really aren't doing anything wrong; they're just doing the role that they're doing. But the girls have a completely different experience. And they lose their whole brain space."

I want to believe I'm much more savvy than I was half a lifetime ago, but still it floored me to ponder that it had never occurred to me that what I had considered to be a personal failing was a systemic problem that plenty of thinkers before me had identified and examined. I had been stuck in the same trap I was in back before I read *The Beauty Myth*: being so self-centered in a particularly feminized way that I forgot to look beyond myself and question *why* I was the way that I was.

This knowledge does not bring enlightenment. I have not spent the last few years studying neuroscience and ancient Greek. My heart will likely never catch up with my brain when it comes to understanding the political and social contexts behind why I feel the way I do. Over the years I have cultivated so many different ways to hate myself. It still hurts. It will always hurt. But then what?

"Only by learning to live in harmony with your contradictions can you keep it all afloat."

—Audre Lorde, *Sister Outsider*

Here's what I know for sure: I still love all of the songs from my mixtapes even though it's better to sing karaoke about heartache rather than to live it. I still often struggle with what I see when I look in the mirror, but understanding the context from which my body image issues arise makes me feel less lonely (literally, there are so many of us out here!). And I also know that there is great joy in discovering writers who can articulate some of the feelings that I'd been circling but had been unable to put into words.

There is comfort in other people's stories, to learn that I am not the only one aching to move past my own petty concerns. Long after I declined to take an intro-level women's studies course, there is feminism, the kind that makes me feel less alone with all the stupid shit that runs through my head. There is art, so much of which engages with those seemingly useless fixations. There is solace in finding myself in books, and it is through them that I can begin to envision what a better world might look like.

> "This is why I read novels: so I can escape my own unrelenting monologue."
>
> —Carol Shields, *Unless*

# COPAGANDA AND ME

Cold open on two turban-wearing, machine-gun-toting guards opening a door to a secret room that looks like it smells of tobacco and sweat and evil. The room is host to a sinister cabal: dictators and other assorted villains from the 1980s sitting around a conference table, plotting to destroy democracy. It's a who's who of America's enemies: Gorbachev, Arafat, Gaddafi, Castro, guys whose faces we've seen on *NBC Nightly News with Tom Brokaw*, who glower at us from the cover of *Time*. "Killing off the hostages is not sufficient," says the Idi Amin stand-in. "The Americans must be made to suffer."

The Ayatollah Khomeini is ranting about how they must conceive of one ultimate terrorist act to end them all when a servant wearing a humble brown robe and a face covering comes over to pour him a cup of tea. Suddenly the servant very deliberately scalds the ayatollah's hand with the teapot. Oh shit!

The servant rips off his disguise, and there he is: Detective Sergeant Frank Drebin (Leslie Nielsen) of the LAPD, the bumbling cop with a head of shining white hair who so often finds himself in extraordinary situations and who just happens to be on vacation in Beirut. Contrary to everything I understand about international law and police jurisdictions, somehow this American cop is on the case, making quick work of each and every one of the bad guys and kicking their asses in hilarious ways reminiscent of the fisticuffs of *The Three Stooges*. In a matter of moments, Drebin easily deposes the most dangerous men in the world with a few head bonks and a well-placed kick in the balls.

This is the opening scene of the crime spoof comedy *The Naked Gun* (1988), and it showed a generation of kids, including me, that one man can single-handedly save democracy—this one good guy with a gun.

———

WE WEREN'T SUPPOSED TO WATCH TOO MUCH TV IN OUR household, but that didn't stop us. We were firmly in the era of "TV rots your brain," before twenty-four-hour cable news and long before smartphones and social media were invented. Before the internet, television was one of our primary tools for learning about how the world worked, what life was like outside of our middle-class suburban neighborhood.

This was not too long after Don DeLillo published his 1985 suburban satirical masterpiece *White Noise*, a critique of media consumption in contemporary American life, in which pop culture professor Murray Jay Siskind, equal parts pretentious and insightful, says, "For most people there are only two places in the world. Where they live and their TV set. If a thing happens on television, we have every right to find it fascinating, whatever it is." We were too young to have read the book, but if we had, I know we would have agreed. Television was the center of our universe.

My brothers are five years older than me, so as a child, I could never wrest the cable box from their greedy hands, but that was okay. While they squabbled for control of the remote, I was just happy to sit next to them on the couch and watch whatever they were watching. There were Saturday-morning cartoons and the ads for sugary breakfast cereals that accompanied them, after-school specials and 5 p.m. sitcom reruns, prime-time TV shows, MTV to fill in the gaps. Dad commandeered the TV at 6:30 every night to put on the news, the one thing that was ostensibly *good* for us to watch.

And of course there were the movies: comedies that were broadcasted over and over again, which we would watch in different twenty-minute chunks until we'd seen the whole thing many times. Like listening to a song on a repeat, movies that were constantly being replayed on cable channels became ingrained in our consciousness by sheer osmosis. Aside from ending credits, information about the films we were watching wasn't readily available; when we wanted to remember the name of that one actor who played the best friend in that one movie, we had to flip through Dad's copy of *Roger Ebert's Movie Home Companion* to get answers. But by force of sheer repetition, what we were viewing could become a part of us, bleeped-out curse words and all. Some of the movies that are still a part of me: *Weird Science*, *Mannequin*, *National Lampoon's Vacation*, *Gremlins*, *Can't Buy Me Love*, *Overboard*.

My brothers loved a zany comedy as much as I did, but they were also delighted by anything with a fight scene, anything with a villain with a dastardly plot or a hero with a score to settle or a war to be won. They liked *Dirty Harry*, but that Clint Eastwood movie costarring the orangutan was much more my speed. If my brothers were watching something really bloody, like a movie in the Rambo franchise, or too loud and cruel, like the reality TV series *Cops*, I would go to another room and read. I liked books, too; it wasn't an either/or. I just liked to get caught up in narratives that took me outside of myself, as, I think, did they. So off I'd go with my *Baby-Sitters Club* and *Sweet Valley High*; later I got into murder mysteries and various James Patterson series, which are the *Sweet Valley High* of police procedurals.

Like Jessica and Elizabeth Wakefield, the twins of *Sweet Valley High*, my brothers, Seth and Jay, looked so much alike that people had trouble telling them apart. People asked all the time whether I was able to tell the difference between them, as if I hadn't lived with them my entire life and understood on a gut level how they varied. But as we know from media representations throughout history, twinhood is one of the most complicated and intriguing of human relationships, a bond nearly supernatural in its potency. From Jacob and Esau to Tweedledee and Tweedledum, not to mention the Doublemint gum ladies, history showed time and time again that twins can be best friends or worst enemies, or, more likely, both at the same time.

Unlike Jessica and Elizabeth Wakefield, my brothers, Seth and Jay, did not have personalities that were as different as night and day. They were more alike than they liked to think. They were both super friendly like my mom, capable of talking to just about anyone, while I tended to shrink back. And they were mostly into the same things: soccer and Little League, hogging the Nintendo, and later, weight lifting. There were smaller differences I could pick up on: Seth was more likely to crack a joke, and Jay was quicker with a smile, but overall they provided a fairly unified front to the outside world. They both knew how to push each other's buttons, how to artfully deploy the little dig that would hurt the most. And I had a front-row seat.

I was perfectly content to play a minor role in my brothers' twin drama, and when they included me in anything it felt like entry into the most exclusive club. How I loved doing silly dances in the kitchen with them after dinner, riding bikes with them in a little neighborhood gang, pillow fighting. But TV watching—this was our true shared passion.

There were times when the twin drama got too intense. One morning, as they were getting ready for high school, a fight broke out in the bathroom. It appeared they had both picked out the same shirt to wear for the day, and one of them was going to have to change. But who? I didn't see it, but I remember blood spattered all over the sink.

Then there was that one fight in the basement, where we kept the weight-lifting equipment. I'm not sure I ever knew what the fight was about, but I swiftly came to know that weights make for cumbersome yet scary weapons. When my mother couldn't break it up on her own, she called the police, knowing they would help. We huddled on the front steps and waited for them to arrive, so relieved when an officer showed up and swiftly deescalated the situation downstairs. He then gave my brothers a stern talking-to and told them to apologize to our mother for scaring her. They obeyed. They were sorry. I know they were. The police officer's presence simply hastened their contrition. We were so grateful.

It's more than a decade later when I realize what a privilege it is for a mother to be able to call the police on one's own children and know they'll only receive a mild scolding and learn an important life lesson, nothing more.

———

WE WATCHED SO MUCH TV ABOUT LAW ENFORCEMENT THAT in the 1980s, I thought policing mostly involved slamming on the gas pedal and darting through busy intersections while suspenseful music played in the background.

Car chases were as reliable a trope as the maverick officer with his own moral code mouthing off to superiors, or the battle-scarred veteran who's seen it all and just wants to eat donuts and make it to retirement. The camera angle is everything, making it feel like you're doing a ride along with a dashing and ballsy officer in excellent sunglasses, who will do anything to catch the bad guys and look cool doing it. Sirens blare, horns honk, tires skid, and suddenly you're zooming down a narrow back alley, hot on the heels of some bank robbers or drug dealers.

*CHiPs*, an early 1980s series about two California Highway Patrol officers, adds a distinctive new twist to the genre. This time, the cops are on motorcycles. Now they're more lithe, more agile, more able to get up to even more trouble. *ChiPs* was my brothers' favorite. They even had the *CHiPs* merchandise, eight-inch action figures of the show's two stars in their uniforms, with a model of a patrol motor bike, sold separately, perfect for zooming around on the tile of our kitchen floor. My brothers, how they loved to go very fast.

———

DON'T TALK TO STRANGERS. DON'T ANSWER THE DOORBELL if your parents aren't home. Don't get lured into any vans by strange men promising candy. Don't end up like the children on the backs of the milk cartons you read about while eating your sugary morning cereal, or like Dudley (Shavar Ross) in that one special episode of *Diff'rent Strokes* where the kids come face-to-face with a pedophile. Have your parents check your Halloween candy to be sure one of your neighbors hasn't hidden a razor blade inside.

Oh, to be a child in the era of stranger danger. With suburban paranoia at its peak, we were taught to be constantly on alert and not to trust any adults except people we knew—and the cops. Every year a couple of police officers would come to school and give an assembly on safety. You should call the police if ever anyone is in danger, they said, or even if you just have a weird feeling about some grown-up who doesn't look quite right.

The cops were the good guys; everyone knew that. And the township cops really did always make me feel safe. It never even occurred to me that they could be villains. By the time I was in high school, I had seen that Ray Liotta movie in which a cop stalks a woman and makes her life hell, but that was strictly for entertainment. Even movies about bad cops usually have a good cop or two who will save the day.

I had no reason not to trust authority. Authority was the police and the evening news and the three newspapers my parents got delivered every day. We were their target audience. It did not occur to me to consider their biases and blind spots, and certainly, I never bothered to get anyone else's perspective.

Newspapers were not inclined to report on police abuses, and local news made the world look like a dangerous place, with kidnappings and robberies and police bravely fighting on the front lines of the war on drugs that was turning city streets into chaos. In the pre-internet days, it took a lot of effort to find out how the world actually worked. Especially if you had no reason to question the facts put before you. Especially if you were a sheltered kid, living in a New York City suburb. Especially if you were white.

"It's no coincidence that the nation's missing child or 'stranger danger' panic originated in a city that much of the nation had already come to regard as the epicenter of dangerous strangers—and a city that had already begun to lay the groundwork to respond with more police and prisons," writes Meagan Day in a 2020 *Jacobin* piece about the moral panic of the 1980s.[*] "The link between mass incarceration and violence against children was there from the beginning of the stranger danger panic, foreshadowing what would transpire in the decades to come."

In *When Crack Was King: A People's History of a Misunderstood Era*, Donovan X. Ramsey recounts how Ronald Reagan's so-called war on drugs of the 1980s did very little to actually help the victims of the crack epidemic, but it did succeed in creating a panic around crime in inner cities. "While Reagan had failed to create a drug-free America, he'd succeeded wildly in drug politics," writes Ramsey. "He did so by conflating the nation's legitimate fear of rising crime with its anxieties about increased drug use. The undercurrent to both, of course, seemed to be lingering hostility toward people and communities of color."[†]

---

[*]  Meagan Day, "How the 'Stranger Danger' Panic of the 1980s Helped Give Rise to Mass Incarceration," *Jacobin*, May 18, 2020.
[†]  Donovan X. Ramsey, *When Crack Was King: A People's History of a Misunderstood Era* (New York: One World, 2023), 219.

To those of us safe at home watching news reports about ruthless drug dealers and crack dens on TV, the streets of New York City looked like a war zone. We clearly needed as much protection as possible, which meant getting more cops on the street. "Taxpayers," notes Ramsey, "happily footed the bill for this war."

———

THE MALE CADETS AND OFFICERS IN *POLICE ACADEMY* ARE just another category of horny goofs, not dissimilar from the frat boys and nerds and caddies and bachelor party attendees that feature in all mid-'80s sex comedies. Even the poster art for *Police Academy* is just *Porky's* but with cops, *Revenge of the Nerds* but with guns: a bunch of misfits with zany expressions on their faces wearing police uniforms, plus one super-hot lady recruit showing some leg and another hot lady recruit with cleavage busting out of her very unbuttoned top. In the corner, peeking out from behind all the cadets, are another pair of legs in sexy platform heels, belonging to someone who appears to be on the ground, possibly for sex reasons. Tagline: "What an institution!"

The series—six films which were made in the 1980s, and the seventh in 1994—really is the ultimate love letter to the institution of policing. It's an ongoing story about how a bunch of weirdos and losers (and some hot ladies) find redemption via their commitment to the police academy, after the newly elected mayor of their unnamed city announces that the academy must accept all applicants regardless of height, weight, gender, or education. We follow a ragtag group of misfits—many of whom don't have the size or shape or temperament that we often associate with cops—who seize the opportunity to become police recruits as they learn some discipline and begin to conform to police procedures, and in doing so they gain authority and respect (and some of them also get laid).

The series begins when the man who would become the leader of the misfits, a conventionally attractive rapscallion named Carey Mahoney (Steve Guttenberg), is forced to enter the police academy to avoid going to prison for comically reckless driving. Throughout the movie, he develops a strong moral compass. Good-hearted fuckups can become actual heroes, the film purports, by aspiring to carry a badge. Throw in some boob jokes and lots of cringeworthy shenanigans at a gay biker bar, and you've got a winning franchise. The chaotic Cadet Zed McGlunk, played memorably by Bobcat Goldthwait in the second film of the series, is the ultimate example of what a uniform can do. When we first meet Zed, he's the leader of a dangerous street gang, wearing a leather jacket and gleefully committing crimes. Everyone knows that guys who wear leather jackets are punks, and all punks are uniformly bad, unpredictable, to be feared. But by the third film, Zed has turned in his leather jacket for his police trainee gear, and bam! "Zed is reformed," an officer explains to Zed's roommate in the academy. "He's on our side now." No further explanation required.

We then get to watch Zed and his recruit class take part in training that consists of target practice, karate, boxing, and a bunch of other cool stuff, very little of which real-life police officers actually get to do. It all culminates in a Jet Ski chase with the cadets pursuing kidnappers at high speeds. They succeed, of course, through a mixture of wits, teamwork, and mastery of the

Jet Ski, which apparently all of them possess. The recruits are green, but they are the police, and the police are the good guys, and the good guys always win. The final shot in *Police Academy 3* shows the academy's crest inscribed with the words "integrity," "knowledge," and "courage," as if by simply walking through the doors of the academy, recruits are endowed with all three (and some of them also get laid).

———

I MOVED TO NEW YORK CITY IN 2000, DIRECTLY AFTER college, even though I knew it was unsafe. In the city, people would try to take advantage of me, or so I was told. On the street, everyone was guilty until proven otherwise, or so I was told. Basically, there were rapists and muggers everywhere, just waiting for oblivious young women to fuck up. This was stranger danger part two, for young white women from the suburbs who move to the city.

And so I was vigilant. I carried my keys in a strategic way when walking down the street late at night. I didn't look any fellow pedestrians in the eye. I avoided dark alleys, even considered carrying a rape whistle. I prepared for my daily commute to work as if I were going into battle, closing myself off in the most unfriendly, self-absorbed way. (An uphill battle for me, because smiling has always been my default.)

This fear escalated tenfold when, a year after I moved to New York City, I watched the Twin Towers fall in real time on the TV at my Midtown office. I will never forget the smell of the city as I walked shakily home about an hour later. It was the smell of everything I could possibly imagine in Downtown burning, the photocopiers and fax machines you'd find in an office as well as the people inside.

In a report on 9/11's legacy for the Pew Research Center on the twenty-year anniversary of the attack in 2021, Hannah Hartig and Carroll Doherty note that fear was the norm. "Most Americans said they were very (28 percent) or somewhat (45 percent) worried about another attack. When asked a year later to describe how their lives changed in a major way, about half of adults said they felt more afraid, more careful, more distrustful or more vulnerable as a result of the attacks."*

At the same time, the NYPD was elevated to hero status. In Rudy Giuliani's post-9/11 New York, I would see people stopping cops on the street to say thank you, and the sight would warm my heart. I felt pride for the people keeping me safe in my city, even as they began to erect surveillance cameras and conduct random bag checks in subway stations.

Then on September 16, 2001, Susan Sontag published a sharp criticism in the *New Yorker* on the messages we were receiving from the government and the media, mostly that America was an innocent victim of an attack. She skewered my newly found patriotism. "The disconnect between last Tuesday's monstrous dose of reality and the self-righteous drivel and outright deceptions being peddled by public figures and TV commentators is startling, depressing," she writes. "The voices licensed to follow the event seem to have joined together in a campaign to infantilize

---

* "Two Decades Later, the Enduring Legacy of 9/11," Pew Research Center, https://www.pewresearch.org/politics/2021/09/02/two-decades-later-the-enduring-legacy-of-9-11/.

the public."* I had no problem with that; I was basically a baby sucking my thumb and waiting to be told that everything was going to be okay. But at the same time my world was getting bigger every day. I was seeing more and reading more and meeting new people with backgrounds different from my own. And as I did, I began to question some of the ideas I had taken to be facts: that New York City is inherently unsafe, that strangers are out to swindle you, that we need cops to keep us safe.

Two decades later I would talk to Casey Plett, a trans writer and publisher I admire, who has every reason to don her armor while walking down the street. Still, she makes the conscious effort not to.

"I doggedly, doggedly believe that there is a balance that most of us know in our bones, about a distinction between guardedness and openness," she told me in an interview about her 2023 book, *On Community*, which grapples with both the positive implications and the faults of the way we think about how we connect to other people. "Plenty of people I know in my life who have survived some of the most awful things at the hands of strangers are also some of the kindest people I know to people they don't know."

How much time I have wasted with my irrational fears.

It never even occurred to me, back in the early aughts, that openness could be a choice, a life-affirming decision about the people around you that you made every single morning before walking out the door, that there is strength in trusting and taking

---

* Susan Sontag, "Tuesday, and After, New York Writers on 9/11," *New Yorker*, September 16, 2001.

care of one another. That such care could mitigate the conditions that beget crime.

"We know that in a society where everyone's needs are met we would no longer be able to fear being unable to pay for our healthcare, or losing our jobs and going hungry, or being hurt by desperate, disillusioned people," write Kelly Hayes and Mariame Kaba in their 2023 book *Let This Radicalize You*.* "Yet many of us accept the violence, limitations, and boundaries imposed by the system as though they are natural laws—inalterable, inevitable, and final—and view everyday people as an existential threat to control, contain, and manage."

———

BEING DEEP UNDERCOVER AS A DRUG DEALER IN MIAMI IN the 1980s involves living a lifestyle that you could never afford on a regular cop's salary: fancy clothes, cool cars, fine dining, yachts. No matter how gritty the work is, no matter how much blood gets shed during shadowy dealings in the dark of night, during the day these Armani-clad cops live in a pastel world where the ocean sparkles and chicks on roller skates zoom by in string bikinis.

Our heroes, Detective Sonny Crockett (Don Johnson) and Detective Rico Tubbs (Philip Michael Thomas), speak often about how alienating their work is, how exhausting it is to constantly be playing a role. But they looked so cool it was hard to feel sorry for them. *Miami Vice* was glamorous and visually delightful, like

---

* Kelly Hayes and Mariame Kaba, *Let This Radicalize You: Organizing and the Revolution of Reciprocal Care* (Chicago: Haymarket Books, 2023), 31.

a hyperstylized music video that went on for forty-eight minutes each week. It made fashion icons out of two cops, turning them into menswear gods; as Crockett, Don Johnson even got to wear a Rolex watch and keep an alligator as a pet. In my house, the policing profession had always been associated with power and authority and masculinity, but now there was an extra aspirational angle. I mean, did you see the Ferrari?

———

SLOWLY I BECAME A REAL NEW YORKER, GROWING COM-fortable enough to trust myself and the other people I saw every day rather than being on high alert all the time. It is a remarkably better way to live. And with that trust came the ability to decide things for myself, to determine which lore about New York City was actually true.

I saw very few roving gangs of criminals; none, actually. I saw street harassers who for sure made me feel discomfort in every single part of my body, but never truly unsafe. I saw unhoused people hassled by cops, and I saw subway fare evaders treated like violent criminals. I saw cops gather on the street outside my local bar at 4 a.m., when the drunk people trickled out, ostensibly to prevent fights, but most of the time they just talked to girls.

On a Saturday night in 2008, I came home from a business trip at close to midnight, groggy and jet-lagged, to find crime-scene tape surrounding my building. Before I could enter, a police officer checked my ID and asked whether I'd noticed any disturbances in the building, anything off. Something was wrong, I understood, but other than letting me know it was safe to go in, he wouldn't tell me anything more. I learned the next morning that a neighbor had been murdered by her boyfriend in her apartment. If I had been home, I might have overheard something from that gruesome, unthinkable night. I was glad I had been away.

A few weeks later, I ran into the cop who'd stopped me in front of my building on the night of the murder. I was at my local bar, a place where I usually felt safe and the bartenders knew my drink order. He aggressively hit on me, and I was disturbed by how quickly he was able to go from protector to pursuer. I craved a feeling of security, of knowing someone out there was looking out for me, but it was nowhere to be found. I'd always loved to watch romantic thrillers, but this felt neither romantic nor thrilling.

Only three months following, in December, two on-duty NYPD detectives were dispatched to help a drunk woman get into her home safely. She testified that she woke up in her apartment to being raped by one of the cops; the other one was on lookout duty. Both men were acquitted of the rape in 2011, and the tabloid headlines were as victim-blamey as you might imagine,[*] but I never again instinctively thought to call the police if ever there was trouble. I was so very lucky to have had reason to hold on to that illusion as long as I did.

By the time my friends were bringing books to the People's Library at the Occupy Wall Street protests at Zuccotti Park in 2011, I was no longer shocked by how quick the NYPD were to dismantle it.

---

[*]  Laura Italiano, "'Rape Cop' Mata describes partner's 'flirty,' 'personal' exchange amid the vomit," *New York Post*, May 6, 2011.

These were just my personal experiences as a former suburbanite who was told over and over again as a kid that the cops were the good guys. If the police had become so ugly to *me*, then there could be no way to ever comprehend the evil that they show to others. Stop-and-frisk wouldn't be proven unconstitutional in New York City until 2013, allowing the NYPD free rein to harass and racially profile at will until then, and with only a little bit more discretion afterward. In 2023, the *New York Times* reported that NYPD anti-crime units were still stopping and searching people unlawfully, and almost all of the civilians they targeted were people of color.*

———

I CAN'T OVERSTATE HOW CLOSED OFF I WAS GROWING UP IN the '80s and '90s, even though I didn't know it at the time. There was a whole wide world that was not getting covered in the *New York Times* or on the evening news, and so Xennials like me were only getting to see a small sliver of it. And then the internet came along and there were so many smart voices aside from the ones I regularly saw in the media, and they were accessible to anyone who wanted to find them.

It's often difficult to recall, in the post–Elon Musk era, that for a moment in the aughts, social media became a tool not just for fucking around or for self-promotion, but for citizen journalism and activism. Twitter was vital.

———

* Corey Kilgannon, "N.Y.P.D. Anti-Crime Units Still Stopping People Illegally, Report Shows," *New York Times*, June 5, 2023.

In the aftermath of the non-indictment of police officer Darren Wilson for the murder of Michael Brown in Ferguson, Missouri, in 2014, writer and editor Jenée Desmond-Harris explained how social media changed the way the world saw the protests. "It started with Brown's dead body lying in the street," she writes in Vox.* "It continued with shocking images of confrontations between protestors and an aggressive, militarized police force, as well as first-person accounts of abuse so dramatic as to be almost unbelievable. And so much of it was captured in photographs and videos." This footage often didn't match what the big major networks were showing, at least until some major players started to use Twitter to find sources.

We take so much media literacy for granted these days, but it was revelatory when I first saw a tweet, say, directly comparing the headlines the news media uses when a person of color is the perpetrator or victim of a violent crime, versus the ones they use for white people in similar situations. Or when a trusted Twitter follower broke down a newly published newspaper article line by line to fact-check and to scrutinize the grammar and vocabulary, a true education in dehumanizing tactics like when the passive voice is used (when trying to let the alleged perpetrator off the hook) versus when publications use actual verbs.

Once you see it, it's everywhere.

———

* Jenée Desmond-Harris, "Twitter forced the world to pay attention to Ferguson. It won't last," Vox, January 14, 2015.

Baby-faced newbie cop Tom Hanson (Johnny Depp), nicknamed "Handsome," gets no respect from the criminals he is supposed to be able to control, nor from members of his squad, a bunch of hardened veterans who don't have time to teach the kid how to gain authority.

Hanson is so frustrated that he goes home from work and angrily plays the saxophone about it, which has very little bearing on the plot but seems like an important 1980s detail to include.

Luckily Hanson has the perfect escape hatch: he gets recruited for a very special assignment headquartered at 21 Jump Street, where a team of young-looking cops go undercover as teenagers to fight crime and teach important lessons to the youths of the day, like don't do drugs. Or sell them.

Usually it's only adult actors who get to relive their youth by playing high school students on TV, but *21 Jump Street* gives this magic power to cops as well.

———

New York City during the early days of the pandemic were the scariest ones I've ever known. Before Covid vaccines were available, it felt perilous to go anywhere at all. We could hear the sound of ambulance sirens around the clock. The people working at the bodegas or stocking the grocery store shelves were literally risking their lives every day. And in the midst of all of this devastation and confusion, the only people I regularly saw who did not wear masks while in public were the police officers patrolling the neighborhood. It had become so clear: these people were not on the side of the community.

And then George Floyd was murdered by police officers and the country was inflamed. The Black Lives Matter movement that had begun in Ferguson moved back onto the streets. In tragedy there was also solidarity, with protestors masked and motivated and taking care of one another. But with that brief wave of hope came new footage on Twitter every night of the NYPD acting like bad cops out of a Harvey Keitel flick: cops harassing peaceful crowds, cops kettling activists, cops literally driving a car into a crowd of protestors. It was impossible to view the police as anything more than a right-wing institution that actively fought social progress. As Thin Blue Line flags claiming to represent solidarity with law enforcement became a familiar sight at far-right actions, it grew particularly difficult to separate xenophobia and general paranoia from the police officer brand.[*]

The guys I had grown up believing were fighting on the side of good had officially become the villains. Or they were just hanging out in clusters in the subway stations checking their phones.

It only got worse when former NYPD officer Eric Adams was elected mayor of New York City in 2022 and began doling out a budget for the police that could sustain an entire country's military: $5.83 billion in 2023.[†] Donna Lieberman, executive director of the NYCLU, criticized the city's police-first problem-solving in 2023: "Adams' executive budget sees the NYPD as the driving

---

[*]  Jeff Sharlet, "A Flag For Trump's America," *Atlantic*, July 2018.
[†]  Jules Roscoe, "NYC Mayor Announces New NYPD RoboCop That Needs a Cop to Guard It," Motherboard, September 22, 2023.

solution for too many of our city's most pressing needs. His budget fails to take a proactive approach to public safety, and includes cuts that would make life worse for New Yorkers."*

It's more than disheartening to watch the city become increasingly militarized as education budgets are slashed and social programs lose funding and city libraries can't afford to be open seven days a week.

In *We Do This 'Til We Free Us: Abolitionist Organizing and Transforming Justice*, organizer Mariame Kaba asks, "What would the country look like if it had billions of extra dollars to spend on housing, food, and education for all?" People like her, she says, who want to abolish prisons and police, envision a different version of society and safety, one that's "built on cooperation instead of individualism, on mutual aid instead of self-preservation."†

———

MY BROTHERS GREW UP AND BECAME COPS, BOTH OF THEM. Twin Jewish cops. I know this sounds like a premise for a bad joke, but trust me, I'm deadly serious. And as much as their matching career paths might sound like a winning formula for some 1980s buddy cop film, I'm relieved to tell you that no, they aren't partners; they've never policed in the same department or even the same state.

---

\* Donna Lieberman, "The NYPD is already too big, so cut its budget: What are New Yorkers getting from spending $29 million daily on cops?" NYCLU, May 3, 2023.
† Mariame Kaba, *We Do This 'Til We Free Us: Abolitionist Organizing and Transforming Justice* (Chicago: Haymarket Books, 2021).

From the time we were small children, the news and entertainment media unceasingly told us that the police would bravely save the day no matter what was wrong, and they would also look cool doing it. I don't want to put words in my brothers' mouths, but how could such depictions not be seductive, as if they could choose a career that was a straight path to being a hero every day and getting paid a decent wage with great benefits for it? It took me years and years to be deprogrammed, to look outside of my own personal experiences and my avid TV watching and begin to see something much uglier in its place. But I was once as enamored with the badge as they were.

We had gone our separate ways as we grew up, not that we'd had a ton of similar interests even as children. I grew increasingly bookish; eventually, I would get paid for reading and even for watching TV, as I'd so often dreamed of as a child. My brothers, on the other hand, would get paid for actually doing the profession we'd so admired on TV.

From what I could see, police work for my brothers wasn't like it was in the movies at all. As far as I know, they've never broken up international terrorist rings or worn Armani suits to meet with high-powered drug dealers on yachts. There was a lot more boredom involved in their day-to-day work than we were led to believe as kids, more sitting around and more court dates and more paperwork, the sheer bureaucracy of the whole thing. The hours were weird, especially at first, when they were newbies and had to work nights and weekends. They were tired and frustrated a lot.

Still, there *were* times when they could drive really fast. They looked good in their uniforms. They got a ton of free coffee, probably even some donuts. That's a cliché for a reason. They were naturals at calling cars "vehicles," as in, "Sir, please step out of your vehicle." And they did help people, even if it was by responding to medical emergencies rather than chasing after kidnappers on Jet Skis.

The institution of American law enforcement, though, emphasizes heroism above all else. By becoming a police officer, the fantasy goes, you also automatically become a hero. In the *Atlantic*, the former sheriff of King County, Washington, Sue Rahr, explains how such self-congratulation obscures so many less palatable truths. "My generation of police was socialized in the comforting myth of police as heroes, engaged in a righteous battle," she writes. "We didn't learn the history of how police have been used to maintain order for those in power, such as on slave patrols or through enforcing Jim Crow laws, busting unions, or waging the War on Drugs. The insular culture of policing protects the flattering myth of heroes and keeps the ugly original mission hidden."[*] Such mythologizing of police and the righteous battles they fight means that violence is a key selling point of the profession, and not the kind we'd watch on the carpet in the den when we were little kids, where there was a clear-cut dangerous villain who needed to be taken by force. So attuned are they to potential villains that my brothers still never sit with their backs to the room in a restaurant, as if they're members of Vito Corleone's crew, on high alert with enemies circling everywhere.

---

[*] Sue Rahr, "The Myth Propelling America's Violent Police Culture," *Atlantic*, January 31, 2023.

In the wake of the Black Lives Matter movement when I, like so many others, reevaluated my relationship with depictions of cops on TV, media emphasizing police heroism above all else feels omnipresent. Crimes procedurals are seemingly as popular as ever, with gazillions of *Law & Order* and *NCIS* franchises, and there's also *Paw Patrol*, a popular animated children's show that I like to refer to as Policing for Babies. I don't bother with them, but I was addicted to *Brooklyn Nine-Nine*, the Fox sitcom (2013–2021) that was the first on-screen depiction of cops I'd ever seen that really reminded me of my brothers. The show starred Andy Samberg as Detective Jake Peralta, a charming and genial kind of doofus who clearly got into police work because as a child he, too, had watched too much TV and dreamed of one day saying "Yippee ki-yay, motherfucker" in a professional capacity. With the help of a charming and ethnically diverse array of loveable colleagues, Peralta brings down criminals in entirely bingeable twenty-two-minute chunks.

In 2018, before I and the rest of the world were ready, my friend, Northwestern journalism professor, author, and activist Steven Thrasher, tweeted about the particular dangers of shows like *Brooklyn Nine-Nine*, referring to it as "an interracial police buddy comedy meant to make white & Black cops seem like your friendly neighborhood jokesters (& to culturally gentrify 'Brooklyn' as sitcom fodder)." After George Floyd's murder, the world began to take Thrasher's critique more seriously. In a 2021 article titled "Cops Are Always the Main Characters," the TV critic Kathryn VanArendonk considered *Brooklyn Nine-Nine* anew: "If anything," she writes, "the show's lightness makes it an even more effective way to generate empathy for the police, who come across as sweet, thoughtful people just trying their best. It sanitizes the police."[*]

This is why I loved *Brooklyn Nine-Nine* so much: because it allowed me to pretend that my brothers are part of something good.

Even the most well-intentioned cops are part of a system that is broken. Rosa Brooks, author of *Tangled Up in Blue: Policing the American City*, told a reporter for Vox that we give cops too many jobs. "We expect them to be social workers and medics and mediators and mentors and warriors and counselors, and no one can be all of those things."[†] Without proper assistance in place for the most weak and vulnerable among us, cops are set up to fail. Sometimes I like to fantasize about what life might be like if social workers got the same movie-star main character treatment as cops do.

Over the years I've watched my brothers become more and more indoctrinated into the police mindset. We grew up in the same liberal household, but my brothers are now people who listen to conservative talk radio and complain about "gangbangers" and crime in general. Sometimes I think they don't believe me when I tell them that I feel safe in my neighborhood; I think they prefer to see New York City as a lawless, scary place where violence could erupt at any moment.

They've seen some shit, they would have me believe, and that has informed their way of thinking: that the world is a dangerous

---

[*]	Kathryn VanArendonk, "Cops Are Always the Main Characters," Vulture, June 1, 2020.
[†]	Sean Illing, "A professor became a police officer—and learned what's really broken about policing," Vox, May 19, 2021.

place and that we must always be on guard. Just as the shit I've seen has me veering in the opposite direction, toward community and trying to take care of one another. I feel our common ground diminishing with each passing year, and I have learned to avoid discussing politics with them at all costs. I don't want to know to what extent our viewpoints have diverged. And yet I love them. My brothers are a part of me, and they are also part of a rotten system that no amount of copaganda can reform.

My brothers and I have become such different people over the years, even if we still share an escapist love of TV and films. But when I get up from the couch and look around, it's clear we need fewer aspiring heroes and more social safety nets for all. This kind of fantasy may be less adaptable for the screen, but the ending will be so much more satisfying.

# PANTING WITHOUT RELIEF

**B**izzy is panting. Actually, it's more like she's a step away from hyperventilating. Her tongue is hanging out of her mouth all cockeyed, leaning at a strange angle to the left; it seems so much longer than what she should be able to coil back inside.

Bizzy is nearly sixteen years old, mildly overweight even for a pug, and very charming. She is unafraid of fireworks and thunder, and she loves people and other dogs. Her face is emotive; she would be a perfect model for a mood chart. Her only fear is of being hungry, and on that front, she is utterly terrified most of the time. She will demand snacks right after eating a meal, or in the middle of the night, or when I've returned after I'd just stepped out for a moment to check the mail.

Most days she will slowly but determinedly make her way down the block to the barbershop where they'll give her a cookie for making an appearance, but by the time she's home she's winded like she ran a 10K. Bizzy walks funny, like so many elderly pugs. Her back legs are weak, and she tends to favor her back right leg, which then tends to cramp up. I have become an expert at dog leg massage. I could start a business.

When we adopted Bizzy, she was almost eight years old—we thought she was ancient even back then. We planned on giving a nice retirement to this sweet yet crotchety old lady whose previous owner had moved into assisted living and had to give her up. And we have. Bizzy has a real nice life. And when things aren't so nice, Bizzy and I both take the same anti-anxiety medication. It's delightful.

Today is killer: ninety-two degrees before factoring in humidity. Just like yesterday, just like tomorrow's forecast. Bizzy is smart enough to stand on the cooling mat that I've set down for her, but not quite smart enough to actually lie down on it and let her heaving belly get chilled. Instead, she lies splooted out on the floor, like a pug-shaped chalk body outline.

I've put a bunch of ice cubes in her water bowl, and I reach to apply a cool washcloth to her forehead. Then to my own. Have I mentioned that I am also panting? I share the washcloth between us, back and forth.

Summer used to be my favorite season. When I was a kid, summer was the Jersey Shore's time to shine: there were beaches and pools to conquer, Skee-Ball and miniature golf to play, foot-long hotdogs and black raspberry ice cream to consume. It was as close to paradise as New Jersey ever felt.

Even after I moved to New York after college, I never felt the need to escape the city. Sure, summer in the city always had the stink of hot garbage, and the close air of the subway platforms was never pleasant, but there was a special magic to New York on a summer weekend. The pace of the city felt slower, not as bustling. You could actually kind of . . . relax. There were days when the streets and sidewalks were less trafficky, the parks and other public spaces less full. There were nights when even the most sought-after restaurants that had been written up in all the New York–centric food blogs had open reservations. A long walk on an early August morning could be the ultimate natural stress reliever, no prescription required from psychiatrist or vet.

But as Bizzy and I have gotten older, the summer has become more complicated for us both. As of this writing, 2023 was the hottest summer on record. Brachycephalic (smooshy-faced) dogs like Bizzy, I have learned, are not cooled, as other dogs are, by panting. It turns out that dogs that don't have long snouts are bad at panting, which feels like a cruel joke considering Bizzy spends 90 percent of her waking hours doing exactly that.

These days I've learned to check the dew point before the temperature, to live and die by the dew point and to plan accordingly for me and Bizzy both. Dew point, I've learned, is a measure of how oppressive the air will feel when you're simply trying to run a few errands or meet a friend for coffee. "Oppressive" is the word from the official definition from the National Weather Service. The fact that we are now increasingly and quite literally oppressed by the air around us, even in formerly moderate climates, doesn't bode well for our future. It's almost as if we should be begging our government to *do something, fucking do something!!!* Just take a look at Exxon, that's all I'm asking!

And so today I'm going to take a cold shower, and I might just subject Bizzy to a cool bath in the sink. I know one thing for sure: the two of us are staying in for the rest of the day.

What do you do when the outside world is so treacherous that your eight-hundred-square-foot apartment becomes your only safe space? Well, let's put it like this: people are always asking me how I find time to read all the books I read. So there you go.

———

ONE MINDFUCK ABOUT HAVING A CHRONIC DISEASE IS NOT having a baseline for how other people feel day to day. This is something I wrestle with often but rarely talk about. I'm always wondering if what I feel is "normal," if there is such a thing. If I'm so exhausted at the end of a hot day that I must cancel my plans to sit in front of my air conditioner and drink Gatorade Zero, is that what regular, nondiabetic people feel like, too? Has the heat become more physically taxing for everyone? Or is it because heat interferes so thoroughly with my diabetes that what I'm experiencing is particular to me? Am I just getting older and clunkier? Or is it all of the above, plus the planet is literally on fire, and what does normal feel like anyway?

But I now have access to hard data via my continuous glucose monitor, and the numbers say no, what I'm feeling isn't normal. Ever since I got my CGM, it's been easy to do little experiments. I walk out of my building on a gross day, note my blood sugar, and then start to meander down the street with Bizzy. As we get halfway down the block, I can see my blood sugar start to climb; it's a little higher when Bizzy finally finds a good place to pee, and by the time I wrangle her back home and give her tiny bites of deli-sliced turkey as a treat, it's officially too high.

———

I HAD NO CGM BACK IN THE GOOD OLD DAYS, WHEN WALKing outside during summer didn't make me physically ill, so I have no control figures. Just a feeling in my gut that outside used to be unequivocally Good For Me and now it is very often Bad For Me.

Each time I hop onto Google, I feel both relieved and validated when I find new studies* about how climate change negatively affects people with diabetes. It's not good news by any means that as the world grows hotter my disease becomes more difficult to control. But at least I feel less like a whiner, less like someone who's just overly sensitive and can't hang. Summers are simply more treacherous for me than they used to be. For all of us. There are fewer and fewer safe places with each passing day.

There was a day in the summer of 2023 when the morning sky in Brooklyn turned from a familiar gray to a luminous fluorescent orange by evening, and I realized that checking air quality alerts along with the weather would be a new and essential part of my daily routine. Wildfire smoke had been a West Coast problem I was grateful to have avoided, my reward for putting up with ruinous winters and hurricanes. All that changed within a matter of hours.

It was like we had time traveled back to early 2020, before Covid-19 vaccines were available and people on the street wore masks because every breath was potentially dangerous. We were used to this but a little out of practice. For me, the biggest difference between those locked-down days and that summer of 2023 was Bizzy. We didn't have to worry about Bizzy catching Covid, but this time I knew air quality would affect her, too. This time around, I found myself Googling whether there were air filter masks made especially for dogs. Bizzy can barely breathe anyway! She needs help!

---

* Jacqueline M. Ratter-Rieck, Michael Roden, and Christian Herder, "Diabetes and climate change: current evidence and implications for people with diabetes, clinicians and policy stakeholders," *Diabetologia*, March 25, 2023.

There was only one brand of dog mask on the market that summer, one that was originally introduced on *Shark Tank*. This credential did not fill me with confidence. It is called K9 Mask. What creativity. The dog model on K9 Mask's website is a German shepherd who must have a beautiful snout, who looks regal and a bit intimidating even with a big blue covering that obscures most of his face. K9, I learn, does not make a product for brachycephalic dogs, whose breathing is labored even before you start trying to put a mask over their smooshy little noses. Not to mention Bizzy would look absolutely ridiculous in the thing anyway.

I had plans in the evening to attend a fancy book event, but once again I canceled to stay inside with Bizzy. Better for us old ladies to stay inside and reminisce about the good old days.

"Stress" is the umbrella term for just about anything that might complicate my diabetes. I'm not alone. Stress complicates just about every major illness under the (increasingly hot) sun, and what's the solution? The effects of climate change are stressors that, unless something dramatic and miraculous happens, will keep on getting worse over time.

Add to that the stress from worrying about all of those stressors, plus the stress of watching Republican politicians deny[*] that climate change is even a thing, plus the stress of knowing that the US government continues to heavily subsidize the oil and gas

---

[*]  Meil Vigdor, "Chaos Erupts When Republican Candidates Are Asked if They Believe in Climate Change," *New York Times*, August 23, 2023.

industries* that are destroying the planet, and you've got a self-perpetuating cycle of cortisol and woe. Not to mention the stress of having to remind yourself that we need to remain hopeful, that nihilism is not the solution to this particular problem. There are only so many deep cleansing breaths a person can take before you're back to panting like a dog.

———

NOSTALGIA IS A TRAP, I KNOW IT. BUT I CAN'T STOP MYSELF from mourning what my perfect kind of summer used to be. The 1980s in central New Jersey were far from ideal, politically or even environmentally (there was ocean pollution from overwhelmed sewage treatment plants,† followed by a phenomenon known as the syringe tide,‡ when medical waste from Staten Island was found washed up on the Jersey Shore in both 1987 and 1988), but I didn't know that then.

Takanassee Beach Club in Elberon, New Jersey, had all of my favorite things: an ocean to swim in until my lips turned an almost grape shade of blue, Oreo ice cream and Skittles from the snack bar, mom's Playmate cooler packed with PB&Js and cold plums (forgive me, they were so delicious), a big pool to horse around in all day long (except for one hour, between 3 and 4 p.m.,

---

* Richard Valdmanis, "Biden budget to target U.S. fossil fuel subsidies," Reuters, March 9, 2023.
† Joseph F. Sullivan, "Bathers Warned About Pollution at Jersey Shore," *New York Times*, August 24, 1985.
‡ Jeremy Greene, "Hypodermics on the Shore: The 'syringe tides'—waves of used hypodermic needles, washing up on land—terrified beachgoers of the late 1980s. Their disturbing lesson was ignored," *Atlantic*, August 29, 2023.

when splash-averse grown-ups swam very quietly), and lots of my older brothers' friends to chase around and try to kick or kiss, depending on my mood.

It's Labor Day weekend of 1983, my fifth birthday, and we've just finished a barbecue in my honor. It's after dinner now, but it's still sunny, cool enough to require a sweatshirt but warm enough to race around in bare feet. And I have just been given a mind-blowing birthday present: an entire jar of M&M'S that seems almost as big as I am. When you're five and you've been presented with a large quantity of candy, life pretty much can't get any better. And then it did.

My parents turn around and see that I've disappeared from the fortress of umbrellas and towels that make up our section of beach. I have taken it upon myself to cart my kid-sized folding chair and my candy jar across the beach to a small stage that's been erected in preparation for a performance by Jimmy the Lifeguard's band. Not only is Jimmy the Lifeguard built and bronzed and authoritative with an air horn, but he also sings and plays the guitar! This irresistible combination has won him a large and diverse fan base, but I have the distinction of being his number one groupie (my eighty-year-old grandma is a close second). So I sit there, munching my pregame chocolate, waiting for Jimmy to put on a show.

It was exactly the right time to be a tiny exhibitionist: I was too young to be self-conscious, and too full of ecstasy not to let it all out when Jimmy started playing. There's a photo of me wearing a Wayside Elementary School sweatshirt over a little red bathing suit, jar of M&M'S in hand, dancing my little ass off, knowing the eyes of the crowd are on me, smiling as big as a wave at high tide. A small snapshot of a moment when everything was perfect, at least for me. In 2024, my hometown newspaper, the *Asbury Park Press*, reported that the sea level on the Jersey Shore has risen more than eighteen inches since 1900 and continues to rise.* Such rising sea levels mean that floods will grow more and more devastating as beaches continue to erode. How can I help feeling homesick for a time when the place I loved felt like it would last forever? Why wouldn't I want to envision a world in which we all had the chance to be so carefree, at least for a moment?

———

I CAN'T PUT MY FINGER ON A PARTICULAR TIME, A PARTICULAR season, when it first became clear that climate change would change my day-to-day life. Long before Bizzy and I were panting on the streets of New York City, people who live outside the global north had already been experiencing the fallout of northern capitalist support for big oil and gas companies for years. And I, from my vantage of "safety," had watched in horror as weather disasters decimated homes and lives in more vulnerable countries. I listened to people more knowledgeable than me about which aid organizations were trustworthy and made sure to send my donation directly to the ones they recommended, doing my part to help put a Band-Aid on an oozing laceration.

I've done all of the things that are supposed to mitigate climate

---

\* Amanda Oglesby, "Which New Jersey towns will sink under water from sea level rise? Find out on this map," *Asbury Park Press*, May 6, 2024.

change: I recycled, cut back on red meat, used washable metal straws instead of plastic, tried to take fewer taxis and walk instead. Now my body tells me adamantly that my bubble of privilege is bursting, that I am no longer safe. No one is.

We must unite to hold corporations accountable for the environmental damage they've done, says Rebecca Solnit in a 2021 opinion piece about the limits of personal virtue: "Private individual actions don't increase at a rate sufficient to affect the problem in a timely fashion; collective action seeking changes in policy and law can."[*] It would be an act of wild, defiant hopefulness to believe that it's not too late, that all is not lost if we can come together to fight. But if I often succumb to the despair of climate pessimism on very hot days when it's difficult to breathe, then maybe there is also some profane relief in collective mourning.

———

BIZZY IS NOT SO GREAT AT STANDING THESE DAYS. HER nubby back legs begin to separate as if she's preparing to do a split, which I am very certain she is not. Josh and I have invested in many rugs to place on our hardwood floors in order for Bizzy's little nails to gain more purchase as she tries to make her way to the kitchen to beg for cheese.

My knees, meanwhile, have become increasingly crunchy with arthritis. My own gait, never quite athletic, has grown uneven at

---

[*] Rebecca Solnit, "Big oil coined 'carbon footprints' to blame us for their greed. Keep them on the hook," *Guardian*, August 23, 2021.

best. Still, when Bizzy refuses to walk a step farther on the side-walk, I pick up her chunky little body in a big bear hug and carry her home, my knees creaking all the way.

It's soothing to reminisce about the good old days, back when Bizzy and I were still healthy young pups, so indulge me once more: It's a July morning at 8 a.m. We spend an hour walking around the neighborhood, Bizzy sniffing lots of good dog butts and savoring the smell of a pile of compost left out in front of a particularly conscientious apartment building. Close to home, a curious toddler gently pets Bizzy's back. Later that morning, we head to the park to play with Bizzy's friends. Or, mostly, I play with her friends while she begs strangers for cookies. Or maybe we just choose to sit outside at our favorite coffee shop, me with a cold brew and a book in hand, Bizzy with a bowl of water and a greedy look in her googly eyes as she assesses each person walking by for the possibility of ever more treats. I imagine the moments Bizzy most enjoys replaying in her head are the ones about un-expected food, like that one time she found an entire slice of pizza on the sidewalk in front of our building, or when she found an intact chicken nugget on a neighbor's lawn.

But nostalgia does us no good in the present moment. We can't go back. There's only what we do tomorrow that matters. These days, Bizzy and I only begin to feel relief when the days get shorter and cooler and the leaves start to litter the sidewalk. We emerge from the apartment on shaky legs, able to breathe a little easier—at least, for a while.

# HAVING IT ALL WITHOUT HAVING KIDS

When I was a kid, I liked to play capitalism. I worked on the weekends, when my dad's law office was empty and he went in for a few hours to catch up. He would take me with him on a Saturday morning and give me the run of the place. I was a business lady. I would write down thoughts on important legal issues on legal pads and clack away on a typewriter. Sometimes my dad would let me sort the mail and put it in the proper cubbies. Instead of cigarette breaks, I would take a timeout to spin around in circles as quickly as I could on rolling desk chairs.

This is what I thought work was when I was growing up in the '80s and '90s, even though I rarely got to see what happened in the office on regular days, when my father left on weekday mornings wearing a suit and tie and carrying a briefcase. I had a vast pop cultural understanding of the professional world, from office movies like *Working Girl* and *The Secret of My Success*, with women in Reeboks and shoulder pads plotting all sorts of corporate intrigue. There were big meetings and bad bosses and overworked but sassy secretaries; most importantly, there was still time to close the office door and fuck around with a colleague (often literally). I aspired to this kind of yuppiedom with no shame.

I especially loved the opening seconds of the 1987 rom-com *Baby Boom*, with its synthesizers and saxes playing over bustling New York City streets. "Sociologists say the new working woman is a phenomenon of our time," announces the voice-over, and Diane Keaton's character breezes by a secretary, who holds out a cup of coffee prepared just the way she likes it, taking her coat. Diane Keaton was the fancy boss lady I aspired to be. But the moment Diane Keaton's character inherits a baby, I lost interest.

Even in my admittedly lame fantasy world, I instinctively knew that having a child would ruin the whole thing. I didn't even want to attempt to Have It All, as *Cosmo* editor Helen Gurley Brown coined in her 1982 book, *Having It All*, billed as a guide for women who want success in all areas of their life—money, sex, family, career. Can a woman have both a career and a family and not lose her mind? Gurley Brown said, *yes, of course*, but the answer has actually been more like *maybe, kind of, but not really*.

This was before I became aware of how nominally America supports its parents, how healthcare and childcare are still more of a privilege in this country than a right. I wasn't thinking about how little flexibility most workplaces offered, how face time seemed to matter more than actual productivity. I certainly wasn't cognizant of the ingrained misogyny that plagues the working world, that might have allowed women the opportunity to climb to the middle, but almost never to the top. Back then, I just thought Corporate Barbie would look less chic carrying a kid around.

Alas, I did not become Corporate Barbie for a number of reasons (I hate wearing heels, I have stumpy legs, I faced various layoffs, I realized breaking the glass ceiling is a visceral and bloody action—it hurts). In fact, I'm a reverse *Baby Boom*: neither corporate success nor motherhood are in the cards for me, and that's quite all right. But what am I if I don't fall into a neat little category of women's roles in society? What then? Or, as Jenn Shapland puts it so aptly in her 2023 essay collection, *Thin Skin*, "What if I don't want the baby or the briefcase? Why is that *all*?"*

———

"SOME WOMEN MAKE IT LOOK SO EASY, THE WAY THEY cast ambition off like an expensive coat that no longer fits," says the heroine of Jenny Offill's perfect little novel, *Dept. of Speculation*, about women who trade in their creative and professional aspirations for the constraints of motherhood.†

And then Offill introduces a new construct that inspires a multitude of think pieces in the years following the novel's publication in 2014: the art monster. "My plan was to never get married. I was going to be an art monster instead," says Offill's heroine, the mother of a young child. "Women almost never become art monsters because art monsters only concern themselves with art, never mundane things."‡

An art monster, according to Offill's fictional character, is the kind of creative person who gets to be entirely bound up in their work above all else, not held back by parenting duties or other quotidian constraints. Art monsters are the Ernest Hemingways and Vladimir Nabokovs of the world. In my little corner of the internet, composed of writers and poets and musicians, "Can

---

* Jenn Shapland, *Thin Skin: Essays* (New York: Vintage, 2023), 203.
† Jenny Offill, *Dept. of Speculation* (New York: Alfred A. Knopf, 2014), 62.
‡ Ibid., 8.

Mothers be Art Monsters?" discourse became the new "Can Women Have It All?"

Kim Brooks, author of the 2018 memoir *Small Animals: Parenthood in the Age of Fear*, wanted to believe that she could have both; she could be a mom art monster. As she wrote on The Cut in 2016: "Surely, I thought, there was no reason in the 21st century that a person like myself couldn't be a great wife, a great mother, and also the sort of obsessive, depressive, distracted writer whose persona I'd always romanticized."[*] Spoiler alert: she could not. Also in 2016, novelist Rufi Thorpe wrote on Vela about what she saw as the fundamental friction of the mom art monster. "For me, the problem then, is not in some platonic incompatibility between art and motherhood, a conflict between the mundane and the celestial, the safe and the unsettling. The conflict is between the selfishness of the artist and the selflessness of a mother."[†]

And then there's Claire Dederer's *Monsters*, published in 2023, which explores the age-old question of whether we can enjoy the art of people who've done terrible things in their personal lives. But for the copious examples of Male Geniuses Who Behaved Abhorrently in Various Ways (Roman Polanski, Pablo Picasso, Woody Allen, Miles Davis), the sins of many of the women artists she mentions (Sylvia Plath, Doris Lessing, and Joni Mitchell, to name a few) fundamentally involve the abandonment of their children. Being a mom art monster, in Dederer's view of society's mores, is the ultimate sin for women, one best to avoid: "If you are going to be accused of child abandonment when you

---

[*]  Kim Brooks, "A Portrait of the Artist As a Young Mom," The Cut, April 2016.
[†]  Rufi Thorpe, "Mother, Writer, Monster, Maid," Vela, June 21, 2016.

go to work—and, more important, if you are inevitably going to internalize these accusations—perhaps better to skip the children and go straight to the art."*

I don't think that Dederer believes that being a mother or an artist is a dichotomy in and of itself. Maybe women can be both mothers and artists. Maybe it's not either/or, it's both/and. But what if I'm messy and selfish, but neither do I want to work on my career all the time? What if I want neither? By the time *Monsters* was published, I had given up corporate life in order to do creative work full-time for five years. But still, I cannot say I was devoting my life to my art, or that I was in a position to. Receiving a steady paycheck was still more important than following my aesthetic bliss.

I've opted out of being a parent and also out of living the life of the artist. I'm too in love with stability for either of those. So once again, where does this leave people like me outside of the range of other people's expectations? What if I want neither the baby nor the easel, the baby nor the blank page?

—

It wasn't that I didn't want to be a mother at first. Being a mom was something regular people did, and I was a regular person, so eventually I would grow up and have kids. For most of my life I strove to conform. I had no interest in being eccentric or different in any way. I had read about oddballs, or people who

---

* Clare Dederer, *Monsters: A Fan's Dilemma* (New York: Alfred A. Knopf, 2023), 196.

chose alternative paths in life, but I never really believed I'd be one. I spent my twenties and thirties striving both to kick ass at work and to find a partner with whom I could build a standard cookie-cutter American family: I wanted the house, the kids, the dog to play in the yard.

It's not that I didn't want to be a mother, it's just that I knew it wasn't even worth seriously thinking about having children until not only was I in a happy and stable relationship with someone I wanted to spend my life with, but I myself was happy and stable. For far too long I was just getting by day to day, paycheck to paycheck. I was living in a studio apartment. I couldn't be responsible for anyone else. I couldn't even manage to get a dog, and I had always desperately wanted a dog.

Then I got exactly what I had hoped for: a man who made me a better person, a man I could count on, a man with integrity, a man I could split rent with. And it turned out, that was enough. More than enough. I had always expected that when and if I could find such a partner, eventually a switch would flip, and I would suddenly want to procreate. That never happened to me.

My diabetes played a role in that: I had grown up watching *Steel Magnolias*, after all. The 1989 tearjerker features Julia Roberts in one of her first major roles as Shelby, a headstrong young Southern woman who goes ahead with a pregnancy even though her Type 1 diabetes has weakened her body and her doctors have warned her against it. You can guess what happens. Since then, technology has made pregnancy infinitely easier for diabetics to manage, but the image of Shelby sitting in a beauty parlor, having the most dramatic low blood sugar attack I had ever seen, is stuck in my psyche forever. Why take the chance?

It just seems much too difficult to be a parent if you're at all ambivalent. I've watched friends go back to work after only a few weeks of maternity leave, or even worse, friends getting laid off immediately after maternity leave. I've seen parents work incredibly hard, only to give their entire salary over to daycare fees. I've seen friends scrambling to get a last-minute babysitter when an emergency comes up.

I also have friends who say that being a parent is the most important thing they've ever done in their lives, and I love that for them, even though I don't want to be them.

I always meant for my decision to not have children to feel like an ordinary part of modern life, a passive choice rather than a radical act. As I learned by watching JD Vance run for office in 2024, repeatedly demeaning women who chose not to be parents by calling them "childless cat ladies," as if that was the lowest kind of person you could be, America is just not ready for it yet.[*]

My husband has a joke about one of the many reasons why we don't have children: he holds up our theoretical child to the splendor of our eight-hundred-square-foot Brooklyn apartment and talks about inheritance. "Someday this will all be yours," he says in a *Lion King* voice. "Not the apartment; we rent the apartment. But the furniture will all be yours. If this Ikea shit holds up."

---

[*]  Monica Hesse, "JD Vance's repeated digs at childless women are worse than you thought," *Washington Post*, September 4, 2024.

NOT THAT BEING AN ARTIST IN AMERICA IS A PICNIC, EITHER. I've read countless craft interviews with authors about the struggle to find time to write in between their day jobs and other responsibilities, overscheduled as even nonparents are. In an essay about the myth of the middle class, Alissa Quart, a writer for Literary Hub, a journalist and poet who writes about economic insecurity, laments how artists are told to think of inadequate pay and job precarity exactly as I was taught to feel lucky for my entry-level job in publishing: as a worthy trade-off. "Writers are often encouraged . . . to think a supposedly fair exchange for not being bored out of our skulls—yet another hat trick of neoliberalism, where the more work provides actual meaning in people's lives, the more it's denigrated as hobby or vanity project, which makes it easier to keep labor costs down across the board."[*] Not to mention the corporate consolidation of book publishers and film studios and music streaming services. Suddenly a wide range of artists are part of the corporate world I envisioned as a kid in the 1980s, and they inherit all the challenges and focus on the bottom line and lack of support that come with it.

If we're only just beginning to acknowledge how insufficiently parents are supported in America, then we're not even close to considering the ways that artists are undervalued as well. In his 2018 essay collection *How to Write an Autobiographical Novel*,

---

[*] Alissa Quart, "Cutting Class: On the Myth of the Middle Class Writer," Lit Hub, April 15, 2024.

Alexander Chee gives a piercing critique of the way America treats its artists. "You are up against what people will always call the ways of the world—and the ways of this country, which does not kill artists so much as it kills the rationale for art, in part by insisting that the artist must be a successful member of the middle class, if not a celebrity, to be a successful artist. And that to do otherwise is to fail art, the country, and yourself."*

To be able to make art is a great privilege at a time when even having *access* to art is a privilege. There are book deserts and defunding for the arts in schools and colleges, libraries that are losing their budgets. The devaluation of art of all kinds feels like one of the great existential threats of our time. Choosing to devote one's life to making art feels nearly as risky as parenthood without a net.

I am a fan of doing mundane things, the petty distractions in which art monsters, according to Offill, traditionally do not partake. I love taking long walks and listening to audiobooks, shopping for groceries, talking to my husband in the afternoon about what we're going to eat for dinner. I even enjoy doomscrolling (I feel the need here to credit my friend, the writer Karen Ho, with the invention of this phrase, which now seems to be a fixture of the American vocabulary). I am perfectly content to aspire to be a good friend and community member, to try to experience pleasure, to even let myself be, gasp, a little bit lazy.

I don't want to make art all the time; I'd rather appreciate it.

---

* Alexander Chee, *How to Write an Autobiographical Novel: Essays* (New York: Houghton Mifflin Harcourt, 2018), 258.

And also occasionally watch bad nighttime soaps. I admit it: I'm a childless writer who is often selfish, but not in the good, optimized art-making way.

A month before the first draft of this book was due, I secured a reasonably priced Airbnb in a cookie-cutter Philadelphia high-rise with a rooftop deck and a clunky ventilation system. Josh would be at home watching Bizzy, and I would have no other obligations to hold me back from devoting myself to my art for three days. I would have the time and space to get work done, to read, to think. No distractions.

I ended up watching a lot of TV, including the last two episodes of a murder-mystery show that Josh and I had been watching together at home. This was, I knew, the moral equivalent of cheating on my husband. Yes, I wrote a bit and read a bit and took walks to clear my head and work out problems in my writing, but I can't imagine if that was all I needed to fill my time. I ended up calling friends, sleeping a lot, window-shopping on Walnut Street, getting a martini at a fancy restaurant. I was lonely, too lonely to be singularly focused on my "art," or any other one thing. How embarrassing to have so much free time with no commitments and still fail to be an art monster.

In response to Claire Dederer's *Paris Review* piece, author and activist Rebecca Solnit argued for more nuance: "Lots of people," she writes, "women and men and nonbinary people, are involved in the needs of people they love and still passionately devoted to their art, or the revolution, or their profession."* I want to opt *into*

---

* Rebecca Solnit, "Rebecca Solnit on Women's Work and the Myth of the Art Monster," Lit Hub, December 12, 2017.

a world of appreciating art and loving my dear ones and trying to make positive changes.

—

I'm perpetually astonished to find that marriage is one of the only institutions that has not disappointed me. I know I'm an outlier here, and lots of people find marriage to be oppressive and old-fashioned for many good reasons, but I find that marriage has made me feel freer.

I can't think of a specific story about me and Josh that illuminates why or how I came to be so content, so instead why don't I tell you how it is most nights when we're both home in our apartment relaxing on the couch?

There's Josh with his laptop balanced on his belly typing away (how is he comfortable like this? But he is!) or tapping away at his phone. I'm probably reading a book. Every so often he'll send me a text with a pair of sneakers he thinks are great (for him or for me) or a clip of a basketball play so spellbinding that he needs me to witness it. I send him dog videos in return.

There is Bizzy. If it's a good night she will lie between us on the couch, snoring in a carefree way, her tongue partially hanging out of her mouth. She might smack her lips a few times or grumble if she's having a good dream.

Eventually we'll turn on the TV and watch a show that we'll deconstruct afterward, evaluating its merits and talking shit when necessary. We always seem to laugh at the same things.

Every now and then Josh and I will touch our toes together, a gentle tap. Or one of us will go to the kitchen for a drink and give a quick kiss on the way back. He will say something and I will laugh; I will do a bit and he will laugh. There might be a bit of dancing, with or without music. We do both, rather often.

I keep waiting to feel regret, to be plagued by the knowledge that it's too late for me to bear children, but it never comes. I have rejected the baby, the briefcase, and the easel, but the life I've built for myself is more than enough.

# RECOMMENDED READING

- *The Idiot* and *Either/Or* by Elif Batuman
- *The Boys of My Youth* by Jo Ann Beard
- *How to Write an Autobiographical Novel* by Alexander Chee
- *Monsters: A Fan's Dilemma* by Claire Dederer
- *Bright-Sided: How Positive Thinking Is Undermining America* by Barbara Ehrenreich
- *Girlhood* by Melissa Febos
- *The Dialectic of Sex: The Case For Feminist Revolution* by Shulamith Firestone
- *What We Don't Talk about When We Talk about Fat* by Aubrey Gordon
- *Creep: Accusations and Confessions* by Myriam Gurba
- *Let This Radicalize You: Organizing and the Revolution of Reciprocal Care* by Kelly Hayes and Mariame Kaba
- *Long Live the Post Horn!* by Vigdis Hjorth
- *Meaty* by Samantha Irby
- *Good Talk: A Memoir in Conversations* by Mira Jacob
- *Post-Traumatic* by Chantal V. Johnson
- *Easy Beauty* by Chloe Cooper Jones
- *We Do This 'Til We Free Us: Abolitionist Organizing and Transforming Justice* by Mariame Kaba
- *Doppelganger: A Trip Into the Mirror World* by Naomi Klein
- *I Love Dick* by Chris Kraus

- *The Hard Crowd: Essays* by Rachel Kushner
- *When We Cease to Understand the World* by Benjamin Labatut
- *Real Estate: A Living Autobiography* by Deborah Levy
- *Tell Me How It Ends: An Essay in Forty Questions* by Valeria Luiselli
- *The Big Con: How the Consulting Industry Weakens Our Businesses, Infantilizes Our Governments, and Warps Our Economies* by Mariana Mazzucato and Rosie Collington
- *The Giant's House* by Elizabeth McCracken
- *Savage Appetites: True Stories of Women, Crime, and Obsession* by Rachel Monroe
- *Anagrams* by Lorrie Moore
- *Dept. of Speculation* by Jenny Offill
- *On Community* by Casey Plett
- *Butts: A Backstory* by Heather Radke
- *When Crack Was King: A People's History of a Misunderstood Era* by Donovan X. Ramsey
- *The Collected Essays of Adrienne Rich*
- *The Anthropologists* by Ayşegül Savaş
- *Committed: On Meaning and Mad Women* by Suzanne Scanlon
- *Thin Skin: Essays* by Jenn Shapland
- *Recollections of My Nonexistence* by Rebecca Solnit
- *The Viral Underclass: The Human Toll When Inequality and Disease Collide* by Steven Thrasher
- *Magical/Realism: Essays on Music, Memory, Fantasy, and Borders* by Vanessa Angélica Villarreal
- *The Collected Schizophrenias* by Esmé Weijun Wang
- *Heroines* by Kate Zambreno

# ACKNOWLEDGMENTS

Parts of some of the essays from this book have appeared, in vastly different forms, in previously published articles as follows:

- "My family founded Barneys. Now the great department store is closing." edited by Alana Okun at Vox
- "Where Did My Ambition Go?" edited by Michelle Legro at GEN
- "A Journey With Naomi Wolf" edited by Laura Marsh at the *New Republic*
- "Listening to My Neighbors Fight" edited by Rebecca J. Rosen at the *Atlantic*
- "Cast by Chronic Illness Into a Limiting Role" edited by Sari Botton at Longreads
- "Unlove Me: I Found Love Because I Got Lucky, Not Because I Changed Myself" edited by Caitlin White at *Brooklyn Magazine*

Thank you to Sarah Burnes for your tenacity, your passion, and your friendship.

Thanks also to Sophie Pugh-Sellers and Aru Menon at the Gernert Company, and a special shout-out to Alia Hanna-Habib for invaluable early feedback.

To Sara Birmingham, for believing in me.

To Deborah Ghim, for editing the shit out of me with acumen and wit.

Helen Atsma and Miriam Parker and Sonya Cheuse and Megan

Deans, how lucky I am to have known you first as friends, and then to get the chance to work with you at Ecco.

Thank you to publicist extraordinaire Cordelia Calvert and Nina Leopold.

Thank you to Vivian Rowe for capturing my exact level of rage in the book's cover design, to fact-checker Joanna Arcieri (yes, of course I paid to get my book fact-checked by a professional!) and to copyeditor Janet Rosenberg.

To my writing group: Glynnis MacNichol, Jen Doll, Kate McKean, Michelle Ruiz, and Carolyn Murnick.

Heaps of love and appreciation to Jason Diamond and Emily Goldsher Diamond and Lulu, Jami Attenberg, Bex Schwartz, Rachel Fershleiser, Rachel Syme, Isle McElroy, Isaac Fitzgerald, Alexander Chee, Caroline Casey, Miwa Messer, Ami Greko, Steph Opitz, Amanda Bullock, Alison Leiby, Lindsey Adler, Adam Dalva, Steven Thrasher, Julie Kosin, Lyz Lenz, Emma Straub, Helen Rosner, Sarah Weinman. Megan Lynch and Nadxi Nieto, thank you for your friendship.

Thanks to Jonny Diamond and Emily Firetog and everyone at Lit Hub.

Thanks to everyone involved in Authors Against Book Bans.

Much love to David Gondelman, Ellie Lyons, and Jenna Gondelman.

Mom and Dad and Seth and Jay: I hope you can tell, in reading these pages, how much I love you.

Josh Gondelman, you make every single thing better.

In loving memory of Bizzy the Pug (2007–2024) the sweetest, grumpiest little goober in the world.